12 Habits of Valuable Employees

Your Roadmap to an Amazing Career

By Verne Harnish
and Kevin Daum
with Anne Mary Ciminelli

Published by Forbes Books, Charleston, South Carolina.
An imprint of Advantage Media Group.

Forbes Books is a registered trademark, and the Forbes Books colophon is a trademark of Forbes Media, LLC.

Printed in the United States of America.

10 9 8 7 6 5 4 3 2 1

ISBN: 979-8-88750-517-6 (Paperback)

Library of Congress Control Number: 2023920088

This custom publication is intended to provide accurate information and the opinions of the author in regard to the subject matter covered. It is sold with the understanding that the publisher, Forbes Books, is not engaged in rendering legal, financial, or professional services of any kind. If legal advice or other expert assistance is required, the reader is advised to seek the services of a competent professional.

Since 1917, Forbes has remained steadfast in its mission to serve as the defining voice of entrepreneurial capitalism. Forbes Books, launched in 2016 through a partnership with Advantage Media, furthers that aim by helping business and thought leaders bring their stories, passion, and knowledge to the forefront in custom books. Opinions expressed by Forbes Books authors are their own. To be considered for publication, please visit **books.Forbes.com**.

Dedication

For all those who believe good is never good enough,
and are ready to create amazing!

Acknowledgements

The authors gratefully acknowledge:

Merced Cohen

Jack Daly

Aubrey Daniels

Dawn Exline

Justin Hersh

Jun-Hi Lutterjohann

Daniel Marcos, Alex Faust, Oscar Perez,
and the team at *Growth Institute*

Denise O'Bleness

John Ratliff

Carolyn Roark

Juanpedro David Salazer

Kit Sauder

Brad Smart

Grace Soueidan

John Spence

Anna Torres of *IPG*

Alex Van

Quynh Van

Van M. Van

Eileen Wainwright

Doug Walner

Jim Weldon

Adam Witty, Evan Schnittman,
and Beth LaGuadia of *ForbesBooks*

Table of Content

Foreword

When my career began, I wanted most of all to inspire people to build something great. At the time, I wasn't sure how to do that, but I knew I needed a company with a culture encouraging growth, innovation, and loyalty; a place where they embrace the time, energy, and effort of its team members. After all, a company is only as strong as its people.

What I found was a "Career with Heart" at Southwest Airlines. As I rose through the ranks of our People Department, I saw firsthand the value of a true partnership between employees and company. This environment sustains when both sides look out for the best interests of the other. Everyone, regardless of position or tenure, preserves and invigorates our culture. That's why Southwest calls our employees "Cohearts," as they are the Heart of Southwest.

Above all else, Southwest recruits for attitude. Our people go the extra mile for each other and for our customers. They identify strongly with the core values that guide the thousands of decisions made at any one time across the company. They strive to provide first-rate hospitality. This attitude gets results: every action by every employee keeps our customers safe, on their way to their destinations, and with smiles on their faces.

The people-centric culture at Southwest is not easy to create or to maintain. It takes hard work and focus every single day. Our industry faces many challenges, carries the heavy responsibility of customer safety, and is often at the mercy of forces beyond our control. The nature of the work demands a great deal from employees, physically and emotionally. It's all too easy for airlines and employees to fall into contention, but when you have the right people in place who believe in the mission of the company, most conflict is easily overcome together.

What makes Southwest unique—and uniquely successful—is the mutual commitment between the company and its employees. In my nearly 30 years at Southwest, I've seen what works—what inspires people to push a company to the next level. What Verne, Kevin, and

Anne Mary explain in this book will evoke the same in your employees. The Habits of Desire, Character, Performance, and Influence will guide your employees as they transform your company into something greater than the sum of its parts. But know that this does not happen overnight. Every employee and leader must work at this every day and in every situation—there is no "pixie dust," and everyone from the top down must be on board.

While it may sound impossible, it's no accident that Southwest has 47 consecutive years of profitability without a single involuntary furlough or mass layoff in its history. Southwest has been on the Forbes "Americas Best Employers" list eight times. Our over 66,000 employees move 130 million passengers every year. If you follow the insights in this book, you will become the Southwest of your industry: financially strong with exceptional employees who become the heart of your company and create passionately loyal customers.

Please take to heart the twelve habits in this book. They will make your organization more valuable to the people you serve, internally and externally. Enjoy the journey!

Shari Conaway,
Managing Director, People Department Southwest Airlines

*I've never received a promotion for a
job I wasn't already doing.*

Dawn Exline

Read This First...

The Road to Adequacy...

...will detour you from realizing your true potential. Most team members and leaders think they're reasonably valuable to their company. They see themselves on a path to better pay, promotion, and a trip up the leadership ladder. Their companies, on the other hand, may think differently.

Closing this perceived gap will determine how far and fast you're able to progress in your career. To use an Olympic analogy, it's the difference between merely running a race and standing on the podium.

Before you begin to apply the 12 habits we discuss in this book, it's helpful to understand why there is this perceived value gap in the first place and how to bridge it.

What Is "Just Adequate"?

What is *valuable* is in the eye of the beholder and often subjective. And most people, when surveyed, consider themselves in the top 50%, if not the top 10%, of their peers!

In turn, team leaders who assess the relative value team members bring to an organization often struggle creating value themselves, which often results in confusion and hard feelings when they critique those who work with them.

Much of what is considered valuable behavior and results is relative to what is being achieved at the moment or historically. Many team leaders have come to expect only what we deem as merely adequate performance—team members willing to meet some minimum standard:

- They show up.

- They deliver the minimum requirements for the job.

- They can think their way through basic issues.

- They deliver on time and on budget.

- They do what they are told.

- They get along reasonably with everyone.

- They don't cause problems.

- They create value relatively equal to their compensation.

In an informal survey of leaders, these were the average traits of team members they liked and would rehire. Yet among the best organizations, these are standards of mere adequacy. They'll keep a company going—treading water—but they won't help it advance beyond its competition. And they may be insufficient for a company to survive, let alone thrive, in a fast-changing environment.

Markets today demand more value from employers and employees alike. The employment market is hyper competitive. The best companies prefer to have fewer, better paid, smarter people than a lot more, lower paid, less valuable team members.

Who Is Creating More Value?

First, we're NOT making a statement about your value or worth as a person—we're all valuable as people. Nor are we suggesting that you are not useful to the company. A-players aren't the only employees who add value. This book is about what it takes to create a higher level of what is seen as valuable to most organizations and their leaders.

So, who is creating more value? In short, we advise senior leaders it's those who "wow" us! It's when leaders exclaim, "Wow, that's better than I could have done!" "Wow, I'm impressed they took the initiative to figure that out!" "Wow, they nailed it!" "Wow, they exceeded our expectations by a mile!"

Believe it or not, every moment and every action you take is an audition for greater compensation and leadership responsibilities in a scaling company. Those at the top are constantly evaluating your performance and behavior to see if you have what it takes to take the company to higher levels of success. Senior leadership is so hungry, and often desperate, for people to step up, lead, and add value, that it's easy to get noticed when an employee at any level creates value beyond their expected duties.

These are the standards for team members who deliver value beyond mere adequacy:

- They look to maximize potential and resources.

- They proactively and systematically solve complex problems.

- They create new efficiencies in everything they touch.

- They creatively make everything better than before.

- They inspire and motivate everyone.

- They eliminate obstacles to facilitate peak performance.

- They deliver an exponential return on investment (ROI).

You might feel these rare traits exist mostly in fairy tales (and some business books!). And you may lament that today's companies don't foster or reward such behavior. Sadly, you would be correct, and that is the reason employees delivering this kind of value must be developed, encouraged, supported, appreciated, rewarded—and retained. We address this approach in the book as well.

Let's be real: most people want to advance and make more money, and compensation is more and more tied to the value you create in any position, be it on the front line or as a leader.

In turn, truly valuable employees understand that they ultimately control their own destinies. Blaming leadership for inadequacies will only hold you back in your career. Part of being valuable is recognizing opportunities and executing ways to win in the toughest of environments. For example, the COVID restrictions in place at the

2020/2021 Tokyo and 2022 Beijing Olympics tested the mettle of many athletes, with the most successful accepting the reality of the situation and making the best of it.

Determining Valuable Potential in Yourself and Others

In *Scaling Up*, Verne outlines four criteria for hiring top talent that are consistent with the philosophies of Jim Collins, Patrick Lencioni, Brad Smart, and other experts in the field of company and team performance. These capabilities are useful to organizations so they can search and test for the people who are the best fit.

If you want to advance your career and be the most desirable to the best companies, these four traits will serve you well. Here are the desired capacities, in their order of importance (and also how they'll appear in this book):

Will: Be a Winner, not a Whiner

Will is often defined as a desire to excel, act with courage, persevere, learn, and innovate. Without strong will, nothing else will happen, and nothing else will matter.

The beginning of the employer-employee relationship almost always feels perfect. The employer is excited about all the talent and benefit the employee will bring. The employee is equally excited about taking on new challenges and the promise of a successful career.

About 90 to 120 days later, however, the bloom comes off the rose and reality sets in. Now what seemed perfect to the employer becomes real, and as flaws in the new employee begin to show themselves, concern mounts. And for the employee, what at first seemed exciting and new starts to feel like cumbersome work and much harder than expected.

It's easy to put this sort of change on the employer and blame the company's culture or leadership's inadequacy. While companies are certainly imperfect, surprisingly the ultimate power always belongs to the employee. Leaders may misplace their efforts, but employees have the ability to disengage (or even leave!) when they want. As an employee, you are responsible for your own experience, harnessing your own curiosity for how to bring value and make positive change in the organization. But let's face it: if you don't care—if you don't want success badly enough—then you will never make the effort to bring yourself, and those around you, from good to great.

Values: Know When to Follow, Bend, and Promote

Values represent the cultural rules by which people act and make decisions in an organization. A valuable employee must be willing, and feel comfortable, playing by these rules.

Every company develops these culture rules over time and makes them known either by design or by default. Team members may, unintentionally, impact the culture both positively and negatively. It's better if there is intention behind every decision to align with the company's values.

Only the employee will know whether a company truly fits his or her own values: whether you have the freedom to be creative, and whether you can truly have a positive impact on others in the work environment. But faking it won't help you in the long run. Others will almost always see it eventually, even if you don't.

Results: Failure Is Not a Long-Term Option

Even motivated people with shared values are ultimately ineffective if they can't deliver on desired performance metrics.

There are many well-intentioned people who somehow never seem to deliver the expected results. Lack of performance is so prevalent, many employers will (often wrongly) put up with a lot of negatives from employees who consistently get stuff done. We have seen companies willingly accept tardiness, disloyalty, and personality issues from someone who performs, regardless of the cultural damage he or she may cause.

Everyone has their unproductive moments, but employers are ultimately looking for measurable consistency and self-improvement. Companies crave employees who can discern between working hard versus working smart to consistently achieve the company objectives that matter most.

Skills: Doing What Needs to Be Done

Aside from interpersonal skills, this capacity is the lowest priority of assessment, since most technical and functional skillsets need updating every three to five years. It is difficult and costly for any corporate training department to keep up with technological and organizational changes.

Companies today need employees who can develop and advance their own technical and soft skills, quickly adapting to the changing environment. They must be self-driven and have the will to become masters of their domains. Those who wait to be taught create a burden on the system and slow company growth.

The 21st century skills that matter most, regardless of industry or geography, are:

- **Observation**—Seeing what's happening around you so you can perceive and interpret patterns and anomalies; the willingness and ability to research what you need to learn.

- **Communication**—Connecting effectively with those above, below, and beside you; relaying the information and emotion required to move the team forward towards the common goal.

- **Adaptation**—Reflecting so you can remove yourself as an obstacle; efficiently executing the necessary tasks; leading others so the team can accomplish more than an individual can personally execute.

These skills, properly developed, not only will survive external and internal disruption, but also will put you at the top of the value chain in any working environment.

Creating Value Together

Employment is not a right or a privilege: it is a pact. It is an agreement where there are deliverables and compensation. Many employers and employees like to read into the concept of employment additional requirements that don't actually exist. Beyond the laws that concern health, safety, and fairness, at its foundation, employment is simply work for hire. But many employers—and certainly most employees— would like to think of employment as more.

Entrepreneurs seek people who buy in to their vision and will create a movement. Corporations want loyalty and performance. Achievers want an advancing career and recognition for their efforts and dedication. This does not happen without forethought, effort, and communication from all parties involved.

How You Can Use This Book

The Importance of Habits

According to data from the US Bureau of Labor Statistics, you will change careers on average seven times. Each change will require learning new technology, markets, and capabilities. What you retain is your ability to perform in stressful and dynamic environments.

Scientists say 40 percent of what we do daily is by habit. Building habits that support positive behavior ensures the ability to bring value in any environment. A person's habits also speak loudly to those around them. In *Change Your Brain, Change Your Life*, Daniel G. Amen, M.D., makes the critical point that both healthy and unhealthy habits are contagious. He argues that people with good habits will foster good habits in those around them.

This Book Is Your Value-Building Guide

Each chapter provides a story that exemplifies the line between adequate and valuable. We share insights from our work with thousands of leaders and team members. We list daily actions to help you become the most valuable team member possible. We also provide ways leaders can foster and reward valuable behavior.

Since some of you are both employers and employees, you should keep both perspectives in mind as you progress. Our approach may not guarantee ultimate success every time, but it's much better than guessing in the dark why the desired results are illusive.

Once you truly understand and own the difference between adequate and valuable, you can build habits that will deliver the latter. Team members who consistently embrace and exemplify the habits laid out in this book become A-players by outperforming and outshining their colleagues. Employers who support and nurture these habits will attract and retain employees who will help them excel in the marketplace. The result is a win-win for all concerned.

Here's How to Use This Guide

Each habit is structured as follows:

- A story of adequacy
- Commentary on the difference between being adequate and being valuable
- An alternate ending of how the story works with a highly valuable employee
- A choice of three action steps employees can take to be valuable

- A "Create Immediate Value Today" section that helps you create value right away

- A link where you'll find additional resources and Growth Institute expertise on the habit in the chapter

We're letting you know, up front, that the opening stories in each chapter describe mediocre employees—and initially, you may read them and think the employee isn't so bad! Many of the characters do meet minimal standards and often appear to be quite proactive and positive.

However, in the commentary after, we'll explain why the employee is just adequate and how they could have strived for more. Again, it might not make sense initially. You may experience empathy, sympathy, and perhaps even indignation at our evaluation. This is to be expected. The situations are common, and the demands are high.

It takes some will and skill to engage honestly with the stories and the commentary, and to evaluate truthfully how you can implement the suggestions into your own career. No one can do it for you. Business is not a spectator sport!

You might feel a bit overwhelmed by the 12 habits and 36 suggested action steps (three per habit) in the book. And it's impossible to act on all of them at once anyway. So, choose one. Whichever one makes the most sense or works best for you, try it out. Don't like it? Try a different one. The key is doing something.

One doesn't expect to master (or even be very good at!) a sport with one lesson. It takes a lot of reps and time. In our experience, it takes 36 months to implement these practices if you have the will. Besides, if it were easy, everyone would do these behaviors automatically and be qualified to move up the ladder. So here are some tips:

Work on One Chapter Each Month

- Read the entire book first. Then when you are ready to act, pick one chapter each month—over the next 12 months—to inspire your behavior.

- When you read the stories of adequacy, think about what more you might do. See if you can anticipate the commentary. Highlight the ideas you missed and consider why it did not occur to you.

- Create your own list of action items and put them on your calendar. Create measurement so you know when you have mastered the practice. When you master the entire habit, find a way to reward yourself and celebrate.

- Repeat this process in the following 12 months—reviewing one habit each month and choosing a single action to take. And then do it again. 36 action steps, 36 months. Relax and trust the process, taking it one step at a time.

- Engage with others as you practice these skills. Take what you learn in your process and have conversations with your colleagues. Perhaps have a weekly lunch and set up an accountability group. Together you can discuss the recommendations and find ways to help each other master the habits and grow.

- If you only have time to do the minimum, use the "Create Immediate Value Today" box. Reading one book, experiencing one speech, and starting the conversation each month will add strong value to anyone's experience.

Returning to the Olympics analogy, the difference between competing (or even getting to compete) and making it to the medals podium is often hundredths of a second or centimeter. The 36 suggested actions in this book are your training regimen for becoming a more valuable team member with the ultimate beneficiary being you and your career.

Remember, being valuable and advancing as a leader may seem like it requires a ton of extra time or effort, but mostly it's a mindset.

If you want to be valuable and ultimately a leader, just be one now. Feel like one, think like one, then act like one. The value quickly will become apparent.

A Note to Those Who Already Are Leaders

Supporting employees who look to lead and add value is a significant responsibility. You set the example every day either inspiring or discouraging those on your team. This book has plenty, both in the chapters and in the Employer's Guide to Stimulating Value at the end, to help you foster more value from all your employees. You will win their hearts and minds with more ethos and pathos than logic or authority. Leave "managing" to the books. Instead, coach your team members as people to achieve the success they most desire for both the company and themselves.

The goal, like for Olympic athletes, is to achieve, each day, their personal best. It's not sufficient to have a handful of "employees of the month." You need to support every employee in achieving their personal best each week and each year.

Before You Begin...

We started writing this book six years ago when we discovered that very few employers actually thought their employees were truly valuable. After interviewing hundreds of employers and employees, we laid out the principles in this book.

When we first shared early drafts, we got mixed reactions. Some tried to blame others for the shortcomings we identified; others told us the book was condescending; still others said, "Well it's about time someone said this." It became clear that everyone came to the book with their own perspectives about value as it relates to a career.

One talented employee, AF, helped us understand what was required to get everyone on the same page. AF is a real person—not an AI creation or a fictional representation like the rest of the characters you'll meet in this book. The letter below is his experience, which we hope will help you understand why the insights in this book are useful and important. We thought it would be a great way for you to start your journey to an amazing career.

I Thought I Was Ready

When I was 23, I got my dream job: product and business development at an international media startup. It was a perfect fit for a marketing major right out of business school.

I hit the ground running: working 60-hour weeks, memorizing core values, developing new products, leading my own team, even putting out fires on other teams. By all accounts I was an excellent employee. Company leadership came to me to discuss personnel issues, production bottlenecks, even budget concerns. On my commute and in my personal time I read about the industry, I took personal and professional development courses, and I cultivated a robust network.

For eight years every indication and interaction made obvious that I was doing everything I possibly could to be my best and bring the company to new heights. I helped close sizeable deals, revenue increased by millions of dollars, and our customer base widened. I took pride in my growth and skills, and I kept on the path.

Company leadership praised me and backed up their words with repeated raises and promotions. My colleagues told me they were in awe of my work ethic. I was nominated for industry awards, and other companies tried to hire me away. Validation came from all directions.

With confidence (and perhaps a bit of bravado—fake it till you make it, right?) I lobbied successfully for the opening as Chief Operating Officer. That's when I learned Jim Collins' most important lesson the hard way: I was shown painfully how "good is the enemy of great."

I was positive that I was a valuable employee. Of course, I had made some mistakes over the years, but the benefits I brought surely outweighed any weaknesses. I was fully committed to my new role. As COO my expectation was that I would continue to solve problems as they arose and kindly encourage others to do the same—simple, or so I thought.

COVID hit like a double-edged sword. Our sector initially thrived, and the temporary market dynamics drove revenue and profitability under my watch.

Let me tell you something: nothing hides flaws and risks like success—until it disappears.

Within a year, the market shifted, our growth drained like a bathtub without a plug, and it exposed all the layers of dirt and grime beneath the surface.

Suddenly, the great achievements of which I had been so proud were nowhere to be found. I was doing everything I thought I should be doing, everything everyone else asked me to do, and more—and I was failing.

Under my leadership, talented people were quitting and morale was weak at best. There was never time for long-term projects. The people on my team weren't developing the way they needed. We all were constantly fighting fires at the cost of everything else. I lived in a state of permanent high stress and exhaustion. My private life suffered.

Worst of all, the company was surviving, but not advancing. There were marginal steps, but we hadn't scaled in a meaningful way throughout my tenure. Both the company and I were stuck in a rut of our own making.

How could all my hard work—work that everyone else thought was so praiseworthy—lead to so little?

What was I missing?

After a period of deep self-reflection, I realized and admitted that *I* was the problem. My ego had gotten in the way. All the years of work and sacrifice hadn't amounted to any real movement in the business or development in myself. I'd bought into my own hype instead of honestly evaluating and improving my performance.

I began to understand that my ego was the roadblock and I needed a bulldozer. I engaged a brutally honest mentor, one whom I had shunned previously because every time I spoke to him, he would point out my flaws with little acknowledgment of my successes—something that few others had the insight or consideration to do.

I finally understood that he wasn't against me. In fact, he was earnestly and honestly advocating for my success and ultimately the success of the company. The two goals were perfectly aligned; I just hadn't seen it.

People kept telling me how great I was, and I believed them, but this time (because I was open) when my mentor held up a mirror, I finally saw that I was merely adequate and not truly valuable.

My mentor helped me see and understand that good simply was not good enough. All the reading I did and the development i would say the word split should be courses, but if it's automated, I won't argue. I took never led to substantive changes in my behavior.

Company leadership had to keep coming to me for solutions because I hadn't put systems and process in place that would have avoided the problems in the first place. There was never time for project planning and strategy because I allowed myself to be sucked into every daily drama.

I was at the head of my team, but I didn't lead them. They weren't developing because I didn't take the time to train them and help them grow, lead, and succeed on their own terms. Colleagues congratulated me for putting out fires without knowing that my inattention and lack of discipline had started the fires in the first place.

Everyone thought I worked hard, and I did—but none of us realized that I wasn't working smart.

Once I realized no one was going to save me from the chaos I created, I went to work with my mentor on embracing a new perspective: great achievement requires great change. My team was full of smart, competent people, and once I trained them properly, I could trust them to execute. I fully embraced the "Scaling Up" and "Rockefeller Habits" principles of alignment and rhythm.

No longer would I focus on what was urgent at the expense of what was important. I standardized processes for vetting candidates and onboarding employees to ensure we hired good culture fits and avoided issues down the road. New products only got approved if they would make a measurable impact on key indicators. I instituted accountability through project planning that empowered others to take full ownership of their work.

I stopped spinning my wheels and started taking meaningful action. Self-awareness and accountability would dictate process going forward.

The sessions with my mentor were emotionally challenging, yet deeply enlightening. I learned you can't rely on someone else to show you the truth—they can only hold up the mirror.

I can't set you up with the mentor you'll need at the time you are truly ready, but in their absence, I've found the stories and solutions in this book serve as a good first step toward shedding your mediocrity and reaching your own potential. My mentor and I agree that the insights in this book will help you develop the right lens to create value and take your career from "meh" to amazing.

-AF

It is said that desire is a product of the will, but the converse is in fact true: will is a product of desire.

Denis Diderot

Part I

Will: Habits of Desire

Habit 1: Developing as a Leader

Habit 2: Aligning Vision

Habit 3: Enabling Growth

How is it that some people make getting to the top seem ridiculously easy? If you're like many people, you struggle to accomplish your tasks, manage your home life, and have any time and energy left to decompress from your career.

Often employees complete what needs to be done out of a sense of obligation or responsibility, but that approach often leads to a low bar of mediocrity and slow career advancement.

You may say, "*I want to feel valued.*" "*I want to advance.*" And yet when faced with momentary decisions that determine success, you often choose an alternative.

What do you truly desire in your work life? Respect? Meaning? Success?

It's easy to want, but action only takes direction based upon what's truly in your heart. Do you really want those things? What are you willing to give up to get them? Perhaps the only sacrifice required is your own current state of mind.

Ultimately, people only do what they actually desire to do.

Truly valuable employees are committed to more than just their job. They are truly devoted to their career.

Commitment will motivate you to meet your obligation but generally stops there. It often shows up as adequacy and leads to mediocrity.

People who are devoted show equal enthusiasm for the mundane aspects of their work as they do for the exciting parts. They see each and every action and moment as an opportunity to learn, grow, and advance themselves and those around them.

The habits explored in Part I require a genuine, heartfelt desire to pursue development in oneself and in the company.

As you read the following three habits, consider how the employees align their personal desires with those of the company. What drives the actions that result in mediocrity versus those that accelerate progress and create exponential value for themselves, their teammates, and the company at large?

Habit 1

Developing as a Leader

Jessica was so excited. When she started at SumCo several months ago, she had dreams of someday being in leadership, but she hadn't quite known how to get there. She certainly didn't think she would have five people working for her at the age of 26. When Jessica started at the company, she made sure to put in the extra hours and keep the quality of her work high. As a customer service representative, she knew it was important to make people feel good every time there was contact, so she tried to apply that to her co-workers as well. Kathy, her VP, recognized how hard Jessica was working. So, when Jessica's team leader Rob left the company and Kathy offered Jessica his position, Jessica saw it as a reward for making the right choices.

The new promotion was a real challenge. Immediately, Jessica had more work and responsibility. She had to clean up messes Rob left behind and deal with some dissatisfaction within the team. Business management classes in college never really addressed the specifics of this sort of situation. Still, Jessica was excited and hoped to be respected by her former peers—now direct reports.

Jessica started to realize that her role required a different perspective. When she was a customer service rep, she simply advocated for her customer and her own needs, and found herself frustrated when the company sometimes made decisions that, to her, were so obviously wrong. Jessica's move into leadership quickly demonstrated that decisions were far more complicated further up the ladder. As an employee, she only considered her own situation. As a leader, she saw the need to consider the implications for all those who reported to her, as well as for her fellow leaders and the good of the company. What before seemed like simple decisions now became complex problems with many possible answers. How should she balance limited resources and competing priorities?

Jessica hoped Kathy would guide her thorough the transition from team member to team leader, but Kathy was on the road a lot. When she was in town, Kathy was consistently booked with upper leadership meetings. Jessica tried to get on her calendar, but 30 minutes every two or three weeks was about all Kathy could spare. In those meetings, Kathy asked how things were going and offered a few suggestions if asked. Sometimes Kathy didn't have any suggestions at all, except to say, "Well, sometimes you have to feel it out and find your own way." Kathy admitted to Jessica it was too bad that the company's leadership development program wasn't designed yet, but the leadership team was just spread too thin at the moment. So Kathy offered the support she could to Jessica, but knew that, as with her own experience, Jessica would mostly have to navigate it herself.

Jessica was disappointed the leadership development program wouldn't be established in time to help her transition, but she understood the resource constraints. Eventually, she learned her job by doing. Through trial and error, she started to develop her own techniques to fight fires. She even read some business articles online to pick up leadership tips. She made mistakes, but usually was able to fix the problems and always learned from the experience. Jessica was able to restore peace on her team, and her team's retention rates returned to the company average. She usually made her quarterly goals and generally kept things humming. Her people respected her and she plugged along with little concern.

Taking Jessica
from Adequate to Valuable

Many employers would love having an employee like Jessica. That's why she was able to move up relatively quickly from the front line to leading her first team. To a busy employer, she is what some would call a "set-her-and-forget-her" type of leader. Jessica finds her own path to success for her team and herself. She requires little attention or resources from her own team leader or her company, and she is competent and reliable. In short, she does a decent job.

In our view, however, Jessica is in the middle of the pack. The bar she sets for herself and her team will not meaningfully advance the company's growth.

Jessica's approach to leadership is self-directed by necessity, since Kathy and the company aren't available to offer much guidance in the short term. Jessica focuses on getting the job done rather than on thinking about how she could develop into a great leader. It isn't entirely her fault; Kathy isn't exactly a shining example of how to inspire future leaders. The company clearly needs to work on gathering employee feedback to identify obstacles and opportunities. Rather than taking the time to set benchmarks for Jessica's growth and ensuring she is accountable for those goals, Kathy simply reacts to Jessica's inquiries. Unfortunately, Jessica can't ask the questions she doesn't yet know. Kathy also doesn't offer any recommendations on books, resources, or courses Jessica can lean on in the absence of a company leadership development program.

Despite Kathy's failures, Jessica still needs to be responsible for her own experience. Most companies inadequately train their leadership, and SumCo is no different. It's the truly valuable employees who drive leadership training and development for themselves and others.

Jessica needs the will to learn of her own accord. She needs to explore the world of leadership through multiple books and other media so she can figure out what she needs to know but has never considered. She needs to expand her network of peers and advisors so she doesn't have to rely solely on the knowledge and experience of Kathy, or worse, herself. Leaders must drive their own path to success.

Even if Jessica herself becomes a better leader, she is still short-changing the company. A company gains value on overall growth, not just the growth of one leader. With an outward-thinking approach, Jessica could look beyond her own needs to see how she can help grow her team members into leaders as well.

She can use her own personal growth process to implement formal programs that will benefit company growth. Sure, she might hit resistance from other leaders who complain about a lack of time or resources, or even about change generally, but valuable leaders learn how to overcome those obstacles to move the entire company forward.

Becoming a better leader creates value for the company because:

1. You can better lead by example to help those around you become better leaders.

2. Your consistent, measurable growth practices lay a foundation for progress for the rest of the company.

3. You help generate an internal pipeline of strong future leaders.

Jessica, the Valuable Employee

Eventually, Jessica learned parts of her job by doing, but she realized trial and error was not an efficient way to develop. She got in touch with others in her company who held similar positions and asked them how they grew into the job. She went online and found well-respected books on leadership. Jessica even contacted the head of the local community college's business department for recommendations on other resources.

Since Kathy had so little time for her and the company's leadership development program couldn't launch for a while, Jessica asked Kathy if the company would pay for Jessica to attend a leadership development course. In return, Jessica offered to write a proposal for and launch an interim SumCo leadership program for employees new to supervisory positions. Soon, Jessica made valuable contributions to her team and to the company. Her team was happy and efficient and took her suggestions to read some of her new favorite leadership books. Her colleagues benefitted greatly from the leadership program, and productivity was up companywide. When the company did finally begin to plan its leadership program, SumCo leadership put Jessica on the course development committee. Jessica was a star on the rise.

3 Value Steps Employees Can Take Today

Valuable employees are fully committed to their own personal development, which anyone can cultivate with one of these steps:

1. Learn something.

Leaders commit to continuous learning. According to *Topgrading* by Brad Smart, A-players read on average 24 books per year: 12 to improve in their profession and 12 for fun. Mark Zuckerberg set a goal to read one book every two weeks. Leadership guru Peter Drucker read fiction books to develop savvier people skills. Beyond reading, attend seminars (virtual and/or in-person) and watch TEDTalks on leadership and personal development (we'll recommend several throughout this book). You may not agree with every bit of the content you absorb, but it will stimulate your thinking. Pick up new concepts and begin a growth trajectory. Invest in yourself as a leader, and you'll already be ahead of the curve.

2. Get a peer coach.

You need to gain experience and objectivity from those on the same journey as you. Renowned CEO coach Marshall Goldsmith suggests identifying a peer coach or accountability partner to challenge each other every day to be better leaders, team members, and family members (Google "Marshall Goldsmith peer coach" for a short "how to" document). Reach out in your company or through your LinkedIn network to people who are new to or striving towards leadership. Get together weekly or monthly to share experiences and ideas.

3. Be a "Multiplier."

Liz Wiseman's book *Multipliers: How the Best Leaders Make Everyone Smarter* explains how some people amplify the results of the people around them. Multipliers identify and unlock the innate talents of their colleagues. Examine your own team and consider their strengths. What hidden abilities have been left untapped? Plan for how you can surface and maximize them. Conduct the same exercise for your own talents.

Create Immediate Value Today

- **If you read nothing else, read…** *Care to Dare: Unleashing Astonishing Potential Through Secure Base Leadership*, by George Kohlrieser.

- **If you watch nothing else, watch…** the "TEDTalks: How to be a great leader" series. Pick your favorite first, then watch more.

- **Start the conversation! Here is a practical tip:**

  - **For you:** Notice someone who needs help and help them—then do this every day of your life.

  - **For your leader:** Create a psychologically safe workplace in which employees know their ideas, questions, and mistakes won't be met with punishment or ridicule.

Want more inspiration?

Find more resources on this habit, including expert advice from Growth Institute thought leaders, at *ScalingUp.com/Valuable_Employee_Resources/*

Habit 2
Aligning Vision

PrepaTax, LLC, tax preparation company had 48 branches throughout the southeastern United States and recently surpassed $50 million in annual revenue. In the last annual strategy planning session, the company's executive leadership team decided on a Big Hairy Audacious Goal (BHAG) of achieving $1 billion in annual revenue within 10 years. The leadership team knew they needed a clear plan to achieve the BHAG, so together with their coach, they fleshed out a One Page Strategic Plan (OPSP) and shared it with all the branch leaders.

In the OPSP, executives decided each branch needed to grow 15% in the coming year. As they explained to the branch leaders when they presented the BHAG and OPSP, they calculated that 15% would be the optimal growth rate that the company could handle without outpacing their resources. They warned not to push much over 15% because of resource concerns.

Alex was recently appointed leader of the Pleasantville branch. Almost as soon as Alex began working at the branch, he caught the eye of the senior leadership team. Alex was a natural doer and dedicated to his job. He quickly worked his way up the ranks, and his performance as branch leader so far was everything executives hoped it would be.

Alex was an ambitious guy and saw the 15% growth plan as an important opportunity for him to impress leadership. He knew they were pleased with him, but this was his first big initiative, and he wanted to hit it out of the park. Based on what he'd achieved so far, Alex believed he could reach 25% growth in the coming year.

Alex made a plan and prepared his team for the push. He created scripts for his team to use to increase lead-to-close conversion and designed two marketing efforts specifically targeted for his branch's local market. He wasn't a computer guy, but he taught himself some software maintenance that IT would otherwise have to perform to keep control. He hyped his team with incentives and pushed them to sell, sell, sell!

Despite some bumps through the campaign, Alex was thrilled with the overall results: 27 percent growth over the course of the year! That was 9 percent higher than any other branch.

The corporate marketing and legal teams weren't thrilled with Alex's ad campaign because it didn't use the latest graphics or all the proper compliance terminology. The corporate IT team also had a nasty clean up of mistakes Alex made on the servers. A couple of veteran tax preparers left Alex's branch during the year due to stress, but Alex figured the push was a good weeding out mechanism, and he expected to replace them with better performers at some point.

Alex thanked his remaining team for their efforts and patted himself on the back for setting a high goal and achieving it. Certain he made an indelible impression on the executive leadership team, Alex hoped to be rewarded with higher compensation and a larger role in the expansion plans.

Taking Alex
from Adequate to Valuable

At first blush, Alex's performance seems fantastic. He doesn't just achieve the goal set by leadership—he crushes it by 12%! Alex knows his local market, sees an opportunity, and seizes it. He develops locally relevant marketing material and teaches himself IT skills to avoid burdening the corporate IT team. This is the kind of initiative any great employee would show, right?

Well, not so fast. Alex's results may sound great, but in reality, it is a maverick performance that puts the company at risk. Alex doesn't want to achieve 25% growth to benefit the company. Instead, he does it purely out of self-interest and utterly without regard for the larger consequences.

Setting high goals that are above and beyond expectations is great— but only if those goals fit into the larger plan for company growth. Alex wants to make a name for himself, regardless of the impact on the rest of the company. Further, he totally disregards the explanation from the senior leadership team that 15% growth allows them to avoid over-taxing resources.

Some may love to have a leader who pushes the envelope in production. But Alex's branch is 1/48th of company revenue and yet used four times the resources, keeping other branches from operating smoothly. By ignoring the limit, Alex shows blatant disregard, frustrating his colleagues and leadership, not to mention putting the company at risk on several levels.

Certainly the senior leadership team isn't without blame. They should assure mutual buy-in from the branch leaders into the overall plan. Even a simple alignment meeting with discussion of overall strategy and context serves better than a few memos about limiting growth to 15%. The senior leadership team failed to ensure that the company's plans and performance goals were accepted by everyone. Further, the senior leadership team should have been monitoring progress and checked in with team leaders to make sure all was on track before damage was created.

And make no mistake, Alex does, indeed, do damage. The marketing, legal, and IT teams have to clean up messes Alex makes. Using inconsistent language and imagery likely isn't the end of the company, but it violates marketing best practices, looks unprofessional, and creates more work for the marketing team when they're already undertaking their own efforts to support the 15% growth initiative. And in the highly regulated world of taxes, using improper terminology could have devastating compliance consequences for a company.

Similarly, the IT team has to fix mistakes Alex makes when he tries to manage his own software maintenance. The results could be catastrophic. Alex knows he is not an expert, but decides to manage the problem himself instead of calling in the specialists. What would have happened if he made more serious mistakes? This robs time and resources that put the company short-handed in case of crisis.

Still, Alex's overreach is the more immediate problem. Putting risk aside, he misses an opportunity to work with his colleagues to develop strategies that might work well across the company, instead of just at his branch. He could focus his extra efforts toward developing more efficient processes that would benefit all branches and help the company achieve its BHAG sooner.

Aligning your actions to the company's vision creates value for the company because:

1. It encourages conversations within and across teams to ensure everyone understands and buys into the goals and plans.

2. It allows everyone to discern how to expend time and resources to achieve the company's ultimate goal.

3. It's an opportunity to unlock the skills of teammates, make the sum of the parts greater, and create exponential results.

Alex, the Valuable Employee

Alex was excited about the BHAG and studied the senior leadership team's plan for 15% growth in the first year. Actually, Alex believed he could probably achieve something closer to 25% growth in his branch, if corporate resources weren't going to be so tight. Nonetheless, he understood and accepted the limits they had put in place.

After studying the One Page Strategic Plan, Alex realized he still had a great deal to learn about his industry. His experience taught him a lot about running an individual branch, but he still didn't know much about expanding a business. First, Alex found out more about the tax preparation industry itself: the revenue it generated, its average rate of growth, how many practitioners there were, the many industry regulations they faced, and much more. He also researched the practices of nationwide tax preparation firms and found out what he could about their growth strategies.

Then Alex turned to his colleagues. He spoke with long-tenured branch leaders and those who previously worked at some of the other national tax preparation firms. He found out about past successes and failures and what they experienced. He also talked to the team at his branch and asked them about any challenges they foresaw in the plan.

Alex knew his local market well and had ideas for some unique advertising that could be particularly effective. He developed a plan and a budget and approached the corporate marketing team to get their feedback. After some changes by the marketing and legal teams, the marketing team identified several more branches that might benefit from a similar strategy.

Alex also considered the IT constraints on the company. He knew there were a number of simple problems the corporate IT team had to work on every day that really could be either avoided or solved at the branch level before being escalated to IT. What if IT taught a series of classes about troubleshooting these common problems? One person from each branch could attend and would then be the first stop for help for minor problems. The IT team loved the concept. Over the next six months, they hosted several workshops to empower local branch staff to tackle common IT issues. This saved the IT team dozens of hours over the course of the year, which allowed them to spend more time building capacity to prepare for the planned growth.

Ultimately, Alex's ideas proved valuable across every level of the company. By the end of the year, every single branch achieved their 15% growth goal, and several, including Alex's, exceeded it without any additional resource strain. The senior leadership team noticed Alex's precise, valuable input and invited him to head a committee that would explore employee-generated ideas for efficient growth. Truly, Alex's initiative, long-term thinking, and teamwork helped set his company on the right path towards the BHAG.

3 Value Steps
Employees Can Take Today

Valuable employees understand that everything is an opportunity to improve the company systematically. You can learn to recognize these strategic opportunities by selecting one of these three simple steps:

1. Absorb the vision.
Consider your company's BHAG and Quarterly Priorities. Do you know them inside and out? If not, ask the senior leadership team of your organization—they will be impressed you're interested. Then consider how often you think of them on a day-to-day basis. Post the BHAG and company priorities where you will review them every day.

2. Align your priorities.
With every task throughout your day, consider whether what you're working on aligns with the company's overall vision. Question the priorities you've set for yourself. Are you focusing on what's important, and not just on what's urgent? If you can't tie an activity back to the company's ultimate goal, you need to reevaluate your actions.

3. Enroll your colleagues.
You've got your own efforts aligned behind the company's priorities, but what about your colleagues? Find out whether your colleagues have embraced the company's vision as much as you have. If they haven't, help them understand and then reprioritize their own actions. The best way to learn and remember something is to teach it.

Create Immediate Value Today

- **If you read nothing else, read...** *Building Your Company's Vision* Harvard Business Review article by Jim Collins and Jerry Porras.

- **If you watch nothing else, watch...** *Big Rocks* by Stephen Covey.

- **Start the conversation! Here is a practical tip:**

  - **For you:** Focus on the number-one thing you can do this week to help the company achieve its quarterly goals.

  - **For your leader:** Ask each team member what their number-one goal is for the week and what barriers there are to achieving it. Their answers will provide coachable moments.

Want more inspiration?

Find more resources on this habit, including expert advice from Growth Institute thought leaders, at *ScalingUp.com/Valuable_Employee_Resources/*

Habit 3
Enabling Growth

Isaac loved the food at VeggieHut so much he took a part-time job there in college. The district leader, Diane, thought he had real potential. After he graduated, she offered him an assistant store leader position at the Boulder store. He jumped at the chance. It was way more exciting than a job at his dad's construction company. Diane shared the corporate plans for expanding the chain into other western states. The intention was to open five new stores per year in each of the next five years. Isaac saw his position as an opportunity to get involved early, work hard, and grow with a company he respected.

Now that he was six months into the job, he couldn't be happier. He loved the hospitality industry, had a real chance for a promotion, and—bonus!— ate free every shift.

The staff at the store liked Isaac. He was fun and helpful, and he listened to their concerns. Franco, the store leader, liked Isaac's focus on keeping the dining room and kitchen spotlessly clean. Diane loved his passion for vegetarian cooking and dedication to the customer experience. She made several comments implying he might fill her shoes someday. Isaac arrived for each shift energized and ready to give his best. He had confidence that everybody was in his corner.

Isaac was nervous about their upcoming health inspector visit, though. The previous store leader hadn't maintained the walk-in refrigerator properly, and it was constantly malfunctioning. A busboy had carelessly told the last inspector, "Oh, that thing is always on the fritz!" The official had shut them down right then and there. Both the expensive repair and the public black eye from the temporary shutdown took a toll on the store. As a result, the store had two poor quarters in a row.

From talking to other assistant store leaders, Isaac knew the refrigerators were a problem at other stores, too. VeggieHut installed the same refrigerators in each of their stores. They rarely broke down entirely, which avoided replacement costs, but as they aged, they had problems. There was no predicting when a refrigerator's temperature would jump past the health code limit. The service and repair costs were adding up.

Still, Franco said they could not afford a new walk-in, especially after their recent revenue downturn. Isaac knew he had to do something to make sure the refrigerator was working properly when the inspector arrived. He certainly didn't want the store to fail a health review on his watch. It could damage his career chances if they let Diane down. Plus, Franco would be no fun if corporate was unhappy with the store. None of the classes at VeggieHut Leadership Camp had covered this kind of problem.

The week of the inspection, Isaac got Franco's permission to pay for a preventative refrigerator maintenance call. He scheduled it for later the same day. He opened the Monday staff meeting with a pep talk to stress the need for a high health score. First, he gave the kitchen crew instructions to make hourly checks of the walk-in. "If you see the needle move into the danger zone," he told them, "take it down a few degrees. Don't wait!" Then, he reminded the hosting staff to alert him as soon as the inspector walked in. He closed the meeting with a warning: "Remember what happened last time someone made a careless remark!"

Eventually, the inspector arrived. Everything went according to plan, and Isaac breathed a sigh of relief when the inspector left without making any negative remarks. He didn't really relax until Franco posted the report, though. It was a record high score for their location! Franco and Diane praised Isaac's efforts, and business was able to go on normally. The Boulder store restored its health department reputation and had a solid quarter. Isaac was proud of the role he played and continued to implement the same strategy for each subsequent inspection.

Taking Isaac
from Adequate to Valuable

Isaac is justifiably popular with both his crew and his supervisors. What's not to like? He encourages camaraderie and has a "rising tide lifts all boats" attitude. He's clearly not one of those people looking to sabotage others while trying to get ahead. He cares about the store and never pushes for the sake of arguing or getting his own way.

Getting things done and being popular certainly make Isaac a decent assistant store leader, but he doesn't add much value beyond taking care of daily business. As a rising leader with ambitions of one day climbing to the top of a growing company, Isaac needs to think on a much larger scale.

The fact that the previous store leader lets the freezer fall into disrepair demonstrates serious breakdowns in process and communication at the VeggieHut company. Information is not moving through the company efficiently, and corporate leaders are not solving critical issues. And it appears employee input is not being taken seriously. There also seems to be a lack of concern about customer reaction and feedback. VeggieHut is an expanding chain with multiple stores, each with a walk-in just like at Isaac's store. Therefore, each store has the same potential vulnerability. It's certainly not all Isaac's fault. Yet by making only the quick isolated fix for his store, Isaac simply becomes part of the problem that will inhibit VeggieHut growth, and his own.

Isaac already has the eyes of senior leadership watching him. He knows the company has a desire to grow. Diane describes an expansive preferred future of opening five stores a year, perhaps with Isaac playing an important role. He needs to internalize this goal in his thinking and actions.

Isaac chose this company as his career path. He needs to step up and make large-scale contributions. From day one Isaac must look at the company through the growth lens and ask himself:

- What is being done consistently poorly, according to current standards?

- What are the existing processes, procedures, and behaviors in the company that will inhibit future growth and scalability?

Isaac already has a rapport with Diane and knows her goals. Immediately after the first health inspection, he should address the freezer issue with the store leader and Diane, explaining how this problem likely exists in multiple other stores, too. If Franco is in the way of the preferred future, Isaac needs to address that with Diane as well. Of course, he could be concerned about going over Franco's head, but part of Isaac's responsibility in a leadership position is to work with others in a way that benefits company goals. Isaac shows true value when he helps both employees and leaders perform at their best in order to help the company grow.

Isaac, working with Diane, Franco, and other leaders, could set up a post-mortem discussion on the freezer issue with the objective of creating systems and processes that ensure all required equipment is properly maintained and that no store is ever at risk of a health violation.

If you want to create value for the company, you must:

1. Adopt company growth objectives as your own personal goals.

2. Identify and flag systemic issues that could inhibit growth.

3. Encourage and enable people and systems that support scalability.

Isaac, the Valuable Employee

Isaac understood VeggieHut's growth goals, so he saw the immediacy of the refrigerator problem. First, he put in place a system whereby someone was scheduled to check the refrigerator several times per day. They would record the results, both to make sure it was done and to gather data on the frequency of the issue. He asked Franco for records of the repair costs and some basic revenue numbers from before and after the failed inspection. Then, he scheduled a meeting with Franco and Diane to share his concerns. He explained how widespread the problem was and compared the price of a new, more reliable walk-in to that of maintaining the existing one. He also compared those numbers to the potential lost revenue at each store and within each region due to failed health inspections.

Isaac encouraged Diane to lobby corporate for a capital investment in new refrigerators. Armed with Isaac's refrigerator tracking data and financial numbers, she convinced corporate that the refrigerators were a long-term, expensive problem that needed immediate attention. Now, stores all over were saving money on repairs and passing their health inspections consistently. Isaac had impressed not only Diane, but also the corporate leadership team.

3 Value Steps
Employees Can Take Today

Many employees believe thinking about growth is someone else's job. They have their small patch of territory to cultivate, and rarely look over the garden wall. Companies need smart people who make the company's growth their own personal mission. Good senior leaders are watching for employees who can see beyond the here and now. Try one of these methods to advance the company and yourself at the same time:

1. Learn the whole business.

You likely can't help the company grow effectively if you don't understand how the various parts of the company work. Don't take for granted that you will be given all you need to know in orientation. Become your own trainer. Enlist colleagues in other departments and experienced leaders in your own department to show you the big picture so you understand company cycles and how all the moving parts connect. One helpful routine is going to lunch with someone from another department and learning how what you do impacts them. Soon you'll have a better feel for how your activities fit within the whole business.

If you see something that doesn't work, evaluate the process and find the real source of the problem (we suggest the book *Banish Sloppiness* by Paul Akers). Don't trust that things should be done a certain way just because they've always been done that way. By the same token, don't create change just for change's sake. Do detailed analysis with the pros and cons of how change will impact growth in the long term.

2. Study scalability.

There are plenty of books and articles on corporate growth and innovation. Commit time and effort to learning how companies grow and what keeps them from reaching their potential. Books like Jim Collins' *Great by Choice* provide useful insights. Absorb Verne's tips in *Mastering the Rockefeller Habits 20th Anniversary Edition*. Hit up your mentors and networks for stories of growth and innovation and become a growth information junkie. When problems arise, design a solution that will be expandable. Take each problem as an opportunity to rethink the very process that failed. Step back and think through more innovative ways to make stuff happen. Consider the mechanics of how your solution might work—or not work!—with hundreds or even thousands of people involved.

3. Create growth committees.

You don't have to figure out everything yourself. Enlist other ambitious colleagues in your growth-oriented activities. Start an email list or occasional meeting that shares important internal developments, useful industry research, and foundational books by authors like Jim Collins and Patrick Lencioni. Encourage all employees to think beyond the day-to-day in the way they operate. Within your own team, share some of what you've learned and be a vocal champion of growth so others will make it a regular part of their thinking, too.

Create Immediate Value Today

- **If you read nothing else, read…** *Mastering the Rockefeller Habits 20th Anniversary Edition* by Verne Harnish.

- **If you watch nothing else, watch…** *Developing a Growth Mindset* by Carol Dweck.

- **Start the conversation! Here is a practical tip:**

  - **For you:** Determine one thing you can do this week to tangibly help your company grow.

  - **For your leader:** In your next team meeting, review the company's growth goals and ask your team to evaluate how the group's actions contribute to those goals.

Want more inspiration?

Find more resources on this habit, including expert advice from Growth Institute thought leaders, at *ScalingUp.com/Valuable_Employee_Resources/*

Ability may get you to the top, but it takes character to keep you there.

Stevie Wonder

Part II

Values: Habits of Character

Habit 4: Integrating Core Values and Purpose

Habit 5: Managing Conflict

Habit 6: Driving Excellence

Who are you? No really. When you are by yourself in your home or out in nature, what are the thoughts and feelings you share only with yourself?

It may seem an odd question for a "business book," but your true character will accelerate or diminish your career in deliberate and often surprising ways.

Most like to think of themselves as diligent, cheerful, contributive, and progressive at work. But it doesn't take much more than a tough experience with a team leader, bureaucracy, or difficult customer to turn the potential of a good day into irritation and resentment.

Many people think they can hide their feelings of lethargy, apathy, disdain, impatience, and insecurity. And many can much of the time. But as workloads and responsibilities increase, cracks appear in the facade and the true self appears, often at inopportune moments. These emotions show up in actions of sarcasm, forgetfulness, complacency, blame, disassociation, and quiet quitting. That's when a fruitful path to leadership and success can turn barren and frustrating.

The adequate employee gives lip service to core values, avoids conflict, and may even help processes and systems suck less. All of this keeps the business engine running but does little to grow the company or the employees in meaningful ways.

Truly valuable employees embody the core values and take pride in advancing the culture in meaningful ways. They look at conflict as an opportunity for growth and development and understand its necessary dynamics. The status quo is never an acceptable option for those who choose leadership as a career path.

The habits explored in Part II require awareness of the world beyond your cubicle (or video chat screen). They show how you yourself can contribute to a culture of mediocrity and boredom, or one of excitement and success.

As you read the following three habits, consider how ego and insecurities restrict the growth of both the employee and the company. How do these employees inspire others to move beyond the acceptable standards and into greatness?

Habit 4

Integrating Core Values and Purpose

- *Foster Growth*
- *Communicate Well*
- *Eliminate Drama*
- *Learn From Everything*
- *Be the Expert*

Those five core values were plastered throughout Commnivore Agency's main offices, along with their core purpose to "help all parties understand better." Megan always got a good feeling when she arrived at work, seeing them right by the main entrance. It was, after all, her suggestion to senior leadership to display them often and prominently. For Megan, seeing core values and core purpose first thing inspired her to be her best at work.

Megan had been with Commnivore for five years. As a creative director, she ran a team of eight very energetic and talented people. She believed in the company culture and tried her best to instill it in her team.

Megan recently welcomed her newest employee, Alan, to the team. She searched for Alan long and hard. He was a talented designer with a ton of experience, and she knew he would be even better for the team than Jane, who left for a start up in San Francisco.

Among Megan's responsibilities as a director was ensuring her new team members adjusted well to their new positions and understood the culture of the company. Core Values was always at the top of her list in acclimating new employees to the culture.

In the past, Megan generally found new employees were quick to understand the concepts behind the core values. She always had a special meeting with her new hires where she introduced the concepts and explained how important they were to the company and her team. With Alan, however, she found him not particularly concerned with core values or core purpose. He said the right things at their meeting but didn't seem to lean into them the way others did, instead focusing solely on his main operational tasks. He was talented and seemed like a nice guy, so she hoped he would eventually get on board.

Megan made special efforts to integrate the core values into the work of her team. She started every weekly meeting with a roundtable of stories about how people on and around her team exemplified core values that week. During the meetings, Alan didn't participate much in the core values discussions and couldn't articulate them when asked to share.

After about six months, Alan was performing his job well but continued to struggle with the core values compared to the team. He still couldn't recite them from memory, and his weekly stories were half-hearted and often off point. His obvious lack of effort in this regard started generating eye rolls from other team members. Word also came back to Megan that while Alan was a good performer operationally, he openly ridiculed and scoffed at "this whole core values thing" in team discussions. Megan also noticed that Alan was prone to making the same mistakes more than once, and that he tended to throw others under the bus when something went wrong.

Megan didn't want this to get out of hand. Alan wasn't communicating well, wasn't learning from his mistakes, and seemed prone to creating rather than eliminating drama—violating three of the core values and certainly not working towards the core purpose of helping understanding. She felt she needed to take action before his annual review, which was still another six months out. Megan had invested a lot of time and effort in bringing Alan to the team, and she was concerned he wasn't going to be a good fit.

Two weeks later, Megan sat down with Alan in her office to have a heart-to-heart. She explained to him that the core values were there for his benefit and that they were extremely important. She made Alan a laminated sheet with the core values and core purpose listed so he could post it in his cubicle. She also asked him to change his desktop photo to the company's core values graphic. She then instituted one-on-one discussion with him before the weekly team meetings to make sure he could participate in a positive manner. She ensured he was prepared to describe instances in which a core value was ignored or embodied by another company member or by himself.

Alan heard the concern in Megan's tone and decided he would go along with her request. He started paying more attention to his own behavior and that of others, and soon started to notice core values in action. Within a few weeks, Megan started seeing progress in Alan. He participated more in the core values stories and seemed to take more responsibility if he made a mistake. Megan even felt the experience was a good reminder for her, too, and helped her better embrace all five core values in her own actions.

Taking Megan from Adequate to Valuable

Most people reading this story would see issues of inadequacy in Alan, and they would be right to do so. But Alan is obviously inadequate in his behavior and therefore easy to spot. Some of the team behavior allowing Alan to skirt by is also subpar, but that behavior really stems from Megan, who is merely adequate as a team leader.

The concern with Megan is that despite the signs and talk about core values, there is actually little or no accountability for employees not living core values. An adequate employee may often speak or talk about core values—a valuable employee actively embodies them. Sadly, it's entirely possible that even at the end, Alan is just paying lip service to the core values in order to avoid conflict with Megan. She tells him knowing the core values are important, but never indicates demonstrating them are actually critical to his continued employment at the company. In fact, it's not clear they actually *are* critical to his employment.

Megan does a good job of talking about core values, but like most people, it stops there. She doesn't specify a connection between the desired behavior and the actual work and the company's goals. It isn't until there is clearly a problem that she discusses with Alan his problematic behaviors and how they are related to the core values. Consistently identifying and calling out positive daily core value behavior helps employees reinforce when they are on track, rather than having them wait for correction when they are off.

Megan also puts her team at risk by allowing Alan to openly and steadily rebel against the values. She depends on his work contribution, so she tolerates poor behavior at the expense of team morale and her own credibility. If Megan had been working with the company to recruit consistently—and with core values in mind—instead of recruiting only when she had to replace Jane, she could have hired a better fit the first time or started remedial culture work with Alan immediately when it is clear he isn't a culture fit. This would minimize disruption to her team and send a clear message about the priority of core values.

Worse, Megan lets the issue go on far on too long. Just because the company only holds annual performance reviews doesn't mean Megan can't create her own more frequent team review processes. Then expectations would be set early for her team so they don't procrastinate improving their behavior. Allowing Alan's attitude to continue for six full months before taking action sends a detrimental message to her team and the company as a whole.

Finally, Megan assumes new hires are automatically as emotionally attached to the core values as she is. Unfortunately, many people focus on their own job responsibilities and work in a manner detached from core values and core purpose. Often the company itself hasn't really made the connection. But Megan could develop her own review method to highlight and exemplify core values.

Ultimately, the company is inadequate in introducing and reinforcing core values and core purpose, and Megan fails to notice or correct Alan's shortcomings. She has the right instincts on the importance of core values but is never proactive in taking action or encouraging the company to institute a more robust core values program.

If you want to create value for the company, you must:

1. Embody the core values with every decision and action and look for tangible ways of living them.

2. Recruit others who will elevate the desired culture.

3. Hold others consistently accountable to the values and communicate with them when you see a particularly good or poor performance.

Megan, the Valuable Employee

As soon as Megan found Alan was unwilling or unable to participate in sharing weekly core values stories, she immediately set up a meeting where they reviewed core values. She coached Alan as to why they were critically important to critically important to achieving the company's core purpose and to his continued employment. She instituted weekly preparation sessions with Alan so they could review his behavior and that of others and be prepared for the team meetings.

Megan also noticed that while Commnivore leadership had accepted her suggestion to display the core values and core purpose at the entrance, there was no institutional support for instilling core values. Worse, there weren't any company policies regarding a failure to embody them. She drafted a companywide core values plan: core values and core purpose would be introduced at new employee orientation, where it would be made clear the employee's future depended on embracing them. New employees would receive training on recognizing and articulating core values in action, and they would receive handouts and cards with core values that could be displayed at their desks and stored in their wallets. All leaders would incorporate core values stories into team meetings and, more importantly, tie every praise or reprimand back to a core value.

Megan shared with the leadership team the core values performance review she used with her own employees, and suggested it be adopted as the standard as a way of directly tying core values to compensation. Finally, Megan proposed core values be worked into the recruiting and application process to ensure all new hires would be a strong cultural fit.

3 Value Steps
Employees Can Take Today

Leaders talk about the importance of living core values. In a practical sense, this means aligning ALL your behaviors and decisions with the core values of the firm. In other words, will the action or decision you're about to take support or violate a core value? Like the rules of any sport, core values play the same role inside an organization. And like with all sports, the umpires and referees are there to make sure the rules are followed.

Therefore, taking it a step further, if you see others violating core values through their behaviors and decisions, will you speak up? If you feel comfortable talking privately with the individual, do so. Otherwise, escalate your concern to their leader. Additionally, if you are watching for core value behavior, you will see those who shine as an example. Call it out so others can learn and encourage all to follow that path.

One of the tenets of core values is that they are "No Matter What!" values. Thus, there are only two types of employees: those who actively live the core values and those who detract from the core values (through behaviors and decisions not in alignment with the core values).

Like a player on a sports team who continues to violate team rules, detractors will disrupt the culture daily. They undermine credibility and create confusion on the team. There is no excuse for maintaining a detractor long term. Only employees who proactively embody core values can benefit the company and set examples for other employees to follow.

You don't have to be a leader or the CEO to integrate core values. You can choose to own, demonstrate, and promote the values in the company even when leadership falls short. In fact, not only will leadership appreciate and recognize you for it, but also they may put you in charge of spreading the appropriate behavior across your department or the entire company. Select one of these three ways to get started:

1. Identify your company and personal core values.

If you don't know your organization's core values, ask. This demonstrates your willingness to be proactive and learn more about the organization. It's also helpful to identify your own personal core values. You can then find ways to make connections between the two lists. If your personal core values are at odds with the company core values, you're likely not a fit and should find a work environment that allows you to be at your best.

Understanding your own "shoulds" and "shouldn'ts" may not be easy to figure out, but it's certainly worth your time and effort. Kevin wrote an Inc. column detailing how to determine your personal core values. You can read it at *www.kevindaum.com/cv*.

2. Build core value evaluation into your responsibilities.

Take the organization's list of core values and connect your various responsibilities to a specific value as best you can. Then set measurable performance goals for each. It's not as hard as it sounds. Elicit the help of a leader in the company if you need it. Again, they'll be impressed by your initiative to seek help.

Quarterly, check in on your performance across each core value and pick one on which to focus your efforts. This way you'll keep them top of mind and will audit and improve your behaviors and results systematically.

3. Enlist others in core value behavior.

Valuable employees don't act in a vacuum. You are as much responsible for having the right people on the bus as anyone else in the company. Help your colleagues apply the core values in their work and daily behavior.

One way to do this, whether you are a team member or team leader, is to connect all praise of fellow employees (shared publicly) and all concerns (shared privately) to a core value. For instance, if someone went out of their way to help a customer, you could give them a shout out and say, "and that's what we mean by our core value [*fill in the blank*]."

In turn, if someone decides or acts in a way contrary to a core value, the conversation can be more about how they made their decision in light of the values. Maybe, in their mind, their decision was justified and aligned with their understanding of a particular core value. This provides a teachable moment for everyone and keeps the focus on the values instead of the person.

Stand up for the company when a culture destroyer reveals themselves. It may be uncomfortable to confront the situation, but co-workers are the last line of defense against cultural decay. The more you work together, the more prevalent the culture will become.

Create Immediate Value Today

- **If you read nothing else, read...** *Great by Choice* by Jim Collins.

- **If you watch nothing else, watch...** *Core Values of Culture* by Tony Hsieh.

- **Start the conversation! Here is a practical tip:**

  - **For you:** Learn your organization's core values.

  - **For your leader:** Every time you praise or reprimand someone, tie it back to one of your organization's core values.

Want more inspiration?

Find more resources on this habit, including expert advice from Growth Institute thought leaders, at *ScalingUp.com/Valuable_Employee_Resources/*

Habit 5

Managing Conflict

Everyone told Brin she was lucky to get such a great job right out of college. Her parents were thrilled that the Longville Healthcare Agency had benefits, paid fairly, and promised stability. Now that she was two years in, Brin wasn't so sure. The work itself was fine, but the environment was beyond tense. It was clear from the start that longstanding resentments and feuds percolated all over the office. Over time, things got worse, and now it looked like a departmental war was going to break out.

Brin dreaded work each day. People spread gossip and sent passive aggressive e-mails. Two of the senior employees hadn't spoken to each other in a month. On one memorable Friday, a meeting erupted into an actual shouting match. Brin used to think this kind of thing happened only in sitcoms. Clearly, she had been naïve; now she was stuck trying to keep her head down and delicately refuse to take sides. Even so, she could see how the environment hurt her efficiency. Really, the whole agency was only able to do half the work it needed to complete.

"The worst part," she told her dad, "is that nobody is completely right or wrong, but they can't get over themselves enough to see it. Rudy, for example, has a great idea for using this new software so we can grow into some opportunities that are just a little out of reach right now. But it's complicated and hard to learn. Plus, he has zero tact, so half the staff writes off his ideas just because they're his. The other half thinks it's a good idea, but don't want to be labeled troublemakers like Rudy. That's just one of, like, ten different conflicts. Andy, our boss, has been trying to resolve things for two years, but the negativity and sarcasm keep shutting him down. I don't know if I can take it for much longer."

After he talked her out of quitting immediately, Brin's dad sent her a book on surviving workplace conflict. She read it carefully and began implementing techniques like active mirroring and pausing to elicit more active communication from her colleagues. She took Andy out for coffee and gave it to him. "I know I'm still junior staff," she said cautiously, "but I can see the toxic energy gets to you, too. I know you're trying to be a great boss and I want to support you any way I can. This book helped me so much in the last month, and I highlighted the techniques that made the biggest difference for me. If you want to implement them, I'll do my best to back you up. Just ask."

Andy was clearly surprised and a little doubtful, but to his credit he soon read it. "Let's give it a try," he said. "I'll start by taking people to lunch, two at a time, and use that empathy/impact technique from the book."

Brin nodded. "Starting with affirmation of feelings and then explaining the big picture consequences of negativity? I used it with Margot last week!"

Andy added, "I want you to come up with a new communication plan for meetings, based on chapter two of the book you gave me. Don't tell anyone what you're doing. The two of us will discuss it when it's ready, and I'll use it at the next meeting."

Brin got right to work, hunting for techniques that would keep the mood positive, diffuse bad feelings, and gently shut down negative comments. She e-mailed it to Andy on Monday; he implemented it on Friday, while she held her breath in the back of the room.

And it worked! There was still some grumbling, but Andy was much better able to control the conversation. Over the next several weeks, people became visibly more respectful after their empathy lunches. It was a clear turning point.

Three months later, the agency seemed like a much calmer place to Brin. It would probably never be the ideal work environment, and some of the staff clearly were never going to be BFFs. But at least there was the promise of civility and mutual respect. Brin could live with that.

Taking Brin and Andy
from Adequate to Valuable

There's no doubt Brin is in a tough situation, and it takes some guts to go to her boss with unsolicited advice. A less confident or open leader than Andy might dismiss that kind of initiative from a junior employee. Both Brin and Andy take a risk that pays off by creating a more peaceful, pleasant environment for everyone. Shouldn't that be enough?

We believe real value happens when the underlying issues that fuel conflicts are not swept aside, but rather are brought to light in a productive way—to "face the brutal facts," as Jim Collins suggests. Brin and Andy get their department halfway there by restoring civility, but they miss the chance to encourage innovation and stimulate growth. Half the department likes Rudy's idea for new software. Unfortunately, his lack of interpersonal skills undercuts his ability to get buy-in and keeps natural allies at arm's length. Brin and Andy don't even try to liberate a worthy message from an unsuccessful messenger. What if they guide their coworkers through an open, honest, and respectful discussion? After neutralizing unproductive fear and aggression, the department might reach new consensus that opens the door to greater productivity.

So much company time goes to firefighting and reactive attempts to pacify disgruntled staff members. Employees create value when they assess the root cause of problems, find productive ways to air differences, and make systemic changes that eliminate problems completely. Treating only some of the symptoms does not solve the problem.

As the leader, Andy is probably better positioned than Brin to take on group facilitation and to mediate those discussions that involve the whole department. Nevertheless, Brin has plenty of opportunity in her personal interactions to sound others for ideas, redirect unproductive behaviors like gossip or backbiting, and play devil's advocate. Through active listening and exercising reason, the valuable employee can turn cynics into advocates and fear mongers into champions.

If you want to create value for the company, you must:

1. Commit to respectful honesty and truth telling in your own interactions.
2. Encourage others to speak their minds, while following the rules of civil discourse.
3. Learn to facilitate discussions where all parties can disagree and debate, and then come to consensus on the right action steps to take.

Brin and Andy, Valuable Employees

Andy was glad he found an ally in Brin and, inspired by her candor, decided to use this as an opportunity to change the team dynamic once and for all. After Andy read the book, Brin and Andy brainstormed how to create a productive meeting where the team would confront and work through their issues. Brin and Andy also made a list of known grievances and crafted possible solutions that gave people the opportunity to be heard while ending the conflict. They also developed a list of rules for future conflict that discouraged bad behavior and kept the lines of communication open. Finally, they designed a new structure for their regular team meetings that reinforced strong communication, identified consensus, and reduced conflict.

Andy convened a special team meeting where he gently but clearly explained why the hostility in their environment was no longer acceptable. It was killing productivity, decreasing staff satisfaction, and impacting the bottom line. He specifically called out issues and allowed anyone who desired to address the team, as long as they were calm and factual. Brin was particularly vocal in expressing her empathy and offering ideas to solve problems and reduce conflict in the future. As a first exercise in their new team dynamic, Andy brought up Rudy's suggestion for the new software, and encouraged the team to evaluate the idea on its merits, rather than on Rudy's reputation.

It was a watershed moment for the team and the whole department. The team became far more productive, and the company was able to save time and money. Everyone's job got easier, and the office became a place to share and productively evaluate ideas.

3 Value Steps
Employees Can Take Today

Conflict can be either a culture killer or a culture maker. Select one of these three strategies to turn a negative into a positive for the whole company:

1. Banish "quiet politeness."
Leadership experts, including Patrick Lencioni, insist that healthy organizations value openness and honesty at all levels. So speak your mind—with tact, of course. Practice sharing your ideas or concerns; ask a friend or family member to role-play with you first, if you feel uncomfortable. Concentrate on saying, or writing, your thoughts clearly and in a few short sentences. Avoid prefacing your comments with apologies or other caveats. We strongly recommend Kerry Patterson's book *Crucial Conversations* to learn more.

2. Become an active listener—and teach others.
Books like Mark Goulston's *Just Listen* (in addition to the Patterson book mentioned above) will outline the listening skills useful in effective communication. At subsequent meetings, practice making your own comments according to active listening rules and follow the recommendations for listening to others' contributions.

Help your colleagues follow set rules for facilitation. Help your teammates become aware how the environment is affected by the presence or absence of rules and structure in communication. Volunteer to lead a meeting and put your new skills to use. Mo Fathelbab's quick-read book *Forum: The Secret Advantage of Successful Leaders* can provide you with a structure and rules for facilitating these sessions.

3. Create an "idea circle."
Too often, informal employee gatherings end up being a space for airing complaints. It can be a relief to unburden yourself and get validation from work friends, but in the end it does nothing to help your career or the company.

Instead, start an "idea circle" that meets for coffee or a happy hour. Allow each person to write down a problem or challenge on a card. Then trade cards; reading someone else's submission aloud will take the emotion out of the situation. Then dedicate ten minutes to sharing possible solutions. Between gatherings, do the research either to show that your position is based on more than your own experience or to improve on your own idea.

Using strong emotion to fuel your argument will rarely encourage others to respond in a calm, rational way. Assign someone to play "parliamentarian"—they will call the group to order if any comments get too emotional, personal, or stray from rational, actionable options.

Create Immediate Value Today

- **If you read nothing else, read...** *Crucial Conversations* by Kerry Patterson.

- **If you watch nothing else, watch...**any of the *Five Dysfunctions of a Team* videos by Patrick Lencioni.

- **Start the conversation! Here is a practical tip:**

  - **For you:** What crucial conversation have you been avoiding? Schedule a time to talk with the person (after watching Joseph Grenny's *Crucial Conversations* video).

  - **For your leader:** Same as above!!

Want more inspiration?

Find more resources on this habit, including expert advice from Growth Institute thought leaders, at *ScalingUp.com/Valuable_Employee_Resources/*

Habit 6
Driving Excellence

Angela loved her job working in the marketing department at Evergreen Commercial Construction, a green building company. For her, contributing to the expansion of business opportunities and civic resources in an environmentally sustainable way was both exciting and rewarding.

A few months ago, Evergreen merged with another green building company, which increased their regional footprint and expanded their technical capabilities. Unfortunately, during the transition process, there were some personnel changes. A couple of people were laid off, and it was initially a struggle for the team to keep up communication with customers. As a result, there was a spike in negative reviews on several employment and customer review websites.

"I'm worried this increase in negative reviews could hurt our marketing efforts, particularly at a time when we need to shore up our pipeline due to the merger," said her boss, Jeff, at the next team meeting. "I also understand from the executive team that we may purchase some other companies to further expand our footprint. So we need to have some processes in place to combat any negative coverage. Angela, I'd like to put you in charge of this effort."

Angela went right to work and soon had a plan to present to Jeff.

"I'm proposing a multifaceted approach. We'll assign someone to monitor our online reputation closely. They'll engage with the audience, thanking reviewers for particularly positive reviews, carefully responding to negative reviews and engaging the person privately. They'll create regular posts for our social media channels. We'll also create a weekly blog on our website where we'll discuss our latest projects, industry trends, and what customers should look for in a green builder. Finally, we'll create a weekly podcast for company employees. Tony in IT knows how to record and edit audio, and he agreed to help us produce it."

With Jeff's approval, Angela went to work. She assigned Bonnie on the marketing team to monitor their online reviews and manage the social media aspects. Bonnie embraced the project, responding to every review she could find, flooding their social media with new posts and sharing interesting content, and engaging with followers all the time. Because of her outreach efforts, a few of the negative reviewers actually took down their posts.

The podcast proved a bit more difficult to get off the ground, but Angela and Tony persevered. A few weeks later they released the first episode, hosted by Angela, which highlighted Bonnie's success in implementing their online strategy.

Over the next few months, Angela, Bonnie, and Tony continued their efforts. Jeff was pleased with the results: nearly 50% of the staff listened to the first episode of the podcast. And although the audience tapered off, Angela and Tony created episodes with some useful information and important reminders, particularly about marketing best practices. It was hard to come up with new topics every week, but they always managed to find something. Bonnie wasn't posting as regularly either, but the uptick in bad press had relented, and they'd gained followers during the initial publicity blitz.

Jeff told Angela that the executive team liked what she had done. They were pushing ahead with their expansion plans, and Angela felt she contributed positively to Evergreen's future.

Taking Angela
from Adequate to Valuable

Cultivating and maintaining a solid reputation is one of the most important undertakings for a company. Angela seems to make some headway on the immediate crisis of the bad reviews online. She also gets some initial traction in the form of new followers for the company's social media and a considerable internal audience for the first podcast. Unfortunately, Angela seems to confuse quantity with quality, and eventually falters even in that. Further, she doesn't develop long-term planning with systems and processes that position the company for the future. Her work is short-sighted and lacks strategy.

At the start of the process, Angela never talks to her boss or anyone else in leadership to discover what their priorities are. She jumps right into action and misses an opportunity to help the company highlight its goals and promote its most important initiatives—which also would solve her problem of coming up with topics. Admittedly, Jeff gives no instructions and never tries to engage in the process. His refusal to micromanage seems admirable, but there's a difference between refusing to micromanage and abandoning your team to their own devices—delegation versus abdication. Company leadership also doesn't seem to have reinforced their long-term goals to their employees.

Next, Angela's instructions to Bonnie are not clear enough to create sustainable habits. As long as you follow best practices, it's fine to engage with angry reviewers. But creating a huge amount of content, as Bonnie does, is not a substitute for quality content that engages followers and leads to a steady stream of new followers. Throwing spaghetti against the wall to see what sticks is not a strategy. Worse, there's no indication that any of the new followers convert into customers for Evergreen.

Angela's performance on the podcast is even less inspiring. It's not clear that Angela and Tony are equipped to make a podcast in the first place. Just because Tony knows how to edit audio doesn't mean he understands how to produce an engaging and valuable podcast. Further, is Angela—or anyone else in the company—well-suited to be the host?

Angela engages in almost no planning to structure a program with a clear purpose. Several months into in the effort, Jeff finds the most useful episodes were about marketing—the very department that produces the podcast. That's hardly a formula to engage the wider company.

Similar to the social media effort, the podcast is not structured in a sustainable way. Angela should create a content calendar that maps out months—even a full year—of topics that cover a variety of issues of particular importance to the company.

Finally, Angela doesn't consider the amount of energy it takes to maintain these efforts. Leaving it all up to the marketing department is a fast path to burnout. She misses an opportunity to engage the rest of the company in the social media and podcast creation. Granted they may not be good at media, but they are the domain experts, and should be tapped for their expertise. Doing so gives the rest of the staff a stake in its outcome and, with just a little training, creates new media competencies across the company. Creating content in a reactionary way doesn't help the company build for the future. Instead, the quality quickly falls off and the entire effort becomes a burden to maintain.

If you want to create value for the company, you must:

1. Consider how every action you take could be an opportunity to position the company better in the future.

2. Develop and implement systems and processes that help colleagues develop the best work product possible.

3. Engage the company in creative thinking and activities to expand competencies.

Angela, the Valuable Employee

Angela was excited about the opportunity Jeff gave her, but she wanted to make sure she did it right. Before taking action, she brainstormed about the situation. What were the root causes of the problems Jeff identified? What were some possible solutions? What were the long-term implications of those solutions? She wanted her action to solve the company's current reputation problem while also putting in place a program they could build on.

She spoke with Jeff and members of the executive leadership team about the company's goals. They explained their short- and long-term plans for growth. The negative online attention so rattled them that they wanted to initiate a program to better engage their audiences—both external customers and internal employees. They also wanted to focus on how they could better integrate the companies they planned to purchase.

Angela knew she needed to create communication in a variety of formats that would efficiently spread the message. She put together an outline for a multi-pronged effort. Internally, she designed a weekly newsletter, monthly (instead of weekly) podcast, and quarterly in-person events for employees. These would emphasize the leadership team's plans, introduce and reinforce core values and initiatives, and recognize outstanding performances. Externally, she created a social media plan, wrote a how-to guide for managing negative online reviews, and designed a regular blog that would highlight the company and industry trends.

Bonnie was enthusiastic about social media and Tony had some experience with audio, but Angela recognized they didn't currently have the necessary media skills to develop and deliver a comprehensive approach. They got permission to hire a journalism major from a local college to work part time to create the actual media. The student helped them develop templates and scripts that would develop creative stories and create formatting consistency. She also suggested that every department be responsible for creating a certain amount of content every year. It would spread out the workload, give different departments an opportunity to shine, and help everyone in the company develop media competency

After one quarter, the company's internal and external metrics reflected the impact of Angela's plan. Externally, their social media accounts had slowly but surely gathered followers, but more importantly, their incoming client surveys indicated that a number of new customers had found out about them from their social media posts and blog. Internally, employee morale was up, reflected in their retention rates. The departments loved taking part in the newsletter, podcast, and in-person event, and the content they created was entertaining and useful. The executive leadership team was so impressed by the program Angela put together that they agreed to budget resources towards next year's effort—which Angela would oversee!

3 Value Steps
Employees Can Take Today

Adequate employees work to improve their own effort. Valuable employees take their new knowledge and spread it systematically throughout the company. You can do the same with one of these strategies:

1. Act with the future in mind.

Every action causes a reaction, and valuable employees always consider the possible implications of what they do. Remember to think both short- and long-term. How will you implement the action? Is it repeatable and sustainable?

2. Create templates.

Valuable employees take a reciprocal approach. They don't keep their knowledge to themselves, but rather find ways of sharing their knowledge and helping others put it to use. If you find a better, more efficient, or more thorough way of completing a task, institutionalize it! Create a template, checklist, workflow, or how-to guide for your fellow employees. Existing and new employees will appreciate your effort. And when others do better work, your work becomes easier, too.

3. Engage creative means.

You doesn't have to be an art major to think outside the box. Today we are surrounded with creativity in almost every activity. The average person spends four hours each day exposed to creative media on a device that fits in the palm of their hand. Open your colleagues' eyes to all the ways people are innovating to grab attention and inspire them to apply those ideas to the way they approach their work and communication.

Create Immediate Value Today

- **If you read nothing else, read...** 7 *Habits of Highly Effective People* by Stephen Covey—always a classic.

- **If you watch nothing else, watch...** *The Three "I" Philosophy for Extreme Leadership*, by Robin Sharma. Go to minute 5.

- **Start the conversation! Here is a practical tip:**

  - **For you:** What is one aspect of your work where you could put in more effort and be more excellent at what you do?

  - **For your leader:** Where are you letting an individual or team get by with less than excellent results? Schedule a crucial conversation to see if it's a process or training constraint.

Want more inspiration?

Find more resources on this habit, including expert advice from Growth Institute thought leaders, at *ScalingUp.com/Valuable_Employee_Resources/*

You don't get results by focusing on results. You get results by focusing on the actions that produce results.

Mike Hawkins

Part III

Results: Habits of Performance

Habit 7: Surfacing Issues

Habit 8: Improving Process

Habit 9: Getting Things Done

Few things in business trigger emotions as much as a simple checklist. For some it's a symbol of intimidation or a reminder of how difficult it is to keep up with the requirements of the job. For others it represents an opportunity to reward oneself with a simple check that provides the high of accomplishment, efficiency, and diligence. In truth it is neither demon nor friend—it is simply a tool. It's most useful when it represents depth of thought and observation of process and performance.

So much in the working world is judged by way of the simple checklist. Did they do their work? Did they get everything done? What's missing? For the adequate employee, checking off most of the list in a timely manner is generally enough to warrant a decent evaluation. Of course, it helps if the employee is pleasant as well.

Oh, how business revels in action. So many companies will elevate people of checklist-level action and then wonder why they stall or burn out at higher levels. The reason is simple: adequate employees shy away from depth and thoughtfulness.

The valuable employee sees beyond the checklist, beyond the actions of the day. Rather than falling into the patterns of the way things have always been been done, they approach tasks with curiosity. They seek to improve systems and processes to increase growth and efficiency.

A-players step out of the process mentally to see the world beyond the task. It's a bit like Neo being able to see the Matrix at its core (See the original movie!).

The habits explored in Part III certainly address action and completion, but also support also support inquiry and process improvement. Together they help you identify patterns of excellence and mediocrity. Once you understand how work processes and productivity happen in real time, you can master both to improve both output and harmony.

As you read the following three habits, consider how the employees execute the difference between working hard and working smart. Where do they meet or exceed the mark necessary for real value generation? Where could your own company benefit from curiosity and reprogramming?

Habit 7
Surfacing Issues

Jonathan was a top loan originator for Midstate Capital Finance (MCF). With 15 years of experience under his belt, he was among the best at the company in getting loans approved and making people's dreams of home ownership a reality. MCF was a successful company volume-wise, but they often left process and training up to their experienced loan officers, who were often strongly independent in their work life.

Jonathan's most recent assignment was to take care of Sean and Rebecca Smith, who were shopping loans to purchase their dream home. During their initial meeting, Jonathan explained the entire application process, including all the paperwork and documentation they needed as well as the length of time required for each step in the process. Sean and Rebecca left the meeting thrilled about their experience and hopeful they would finally be able to buy their ideal home.

Jonathan looked through the initial application submitted by Sean and Rebecca and found a few inconsistencies here and there. He explained the issues but assured them their application would be fine. He hadn't seen these exact issues before, but he rarely encountered a problem he couldn't solve.

Mortgage processing got underway. The Smiths sent Jonathan their documentation, and Jonathan ordered the appraisal and title policy as expected. He kept in touch with Sean and Rebecca throughout, assuring them their dream was just a few weeks away.

Still, complications kept arising, and the Smith loan became Jonathan's chief priority in the ensuing weeks. It took up more time than he wanted since he was working on other accounts as well. Always at ease, however, Jonathan got through all his work without major distractions or obstacles.

Then during the underwriting process, Jonathan learned the Smith loan was kicked out of the system due to inconsistencies between the documentation submitted by the Smiths, the sent verifications, and their original application.

In addition, guideline changes just went into effect that meant the Smiths had to come up with more cash than expected toward their down payment. This was the first Jonathan heard of the changes, although they were posted online. The loan might have to be resubmitted, delaying the process and putting Sean and Rebecca's dreams in jeopardy.

Jonathan kept his cool and remained optimistic. This was not the first time he dealt with a situation like this. That afternoon, Sean and Rebecca called to find out what was causing the delay in the approval of their loan. They were beginning to feel unsettled. Jonathan responded with confidence and calmed them. He explained the down payment issue and helped them come up with creative ways to solve it. As the call drew to a close, Jonathan promised Sean and Rebecca that he would do everything in his power to get them into their new home.

Jonathan called the underwriter and went to bat for his clients, fighting every inconsistency allegedly found in the application and backing up his assertions with the documentation he received at the beginning of the process. He went back to the Smiths and asked for verification of the contested documentation, ultimately spending hours with them on the phone. He did his best to ease their worries while he worked to address the underwriter's concerns. Each time he received news about the loan, he immediately alerted the Smiths and the realtors involved in the transaction.

After a few days of hard work, Jonathan realized he was getting nowhere with the underwriter. He decided to go over the underwriter's head to the department supervisor and cut a deal to get the loan done. Jonathan got the deal to close and set up the meeting that finally made the Smith's dream a reality. A week later, the Smiths closed and moved into their new home. A few weeks after that, Jonathan found out two other loan originators at MCF faced the same problem with the recent guideline changes, and ultimately lost the loans—and the clients.

Taking Jonathan
from Adequate to Valuable

In strongly sales-oriented companies, heroics are often lauded at the expense of process. Jonathan's would be the sort of "good behavior" story told at sales meetings for motivation. But as Jim Collins says, "Good is often the enemy of great."

Jonathan is certainly effective at getting the job done and ensuring that Sean and Rebecca get what they want. He leads them through a crisis and delivers in the end—if only by the skin of his teeth.

Colleagues and clients often admire people who achieve success under this sort of pressure. It seems like they are always pulling a rabbit out of their hat at the very last minute to save the day. However, their heroics can cover over the fact that their own behavior caused the need for heroics in the first place.

Jonathan's behavior is mostly reactive. He has a system that works – mostly. He starts the process and then goes to battle. In his view, this method makes his job easier because it requires less thought and work than it would to go in prepared initially. But Jonathan's approach is ineffective. He adds unnecessary stress to his office, his clients, and his vendors. He relies on sheer force of will and the ability to solve crises rather than using preparation and attention to detail to surface issues before they become problems. Ultimately, his method wastes time: fighting avoidable fires takes far longer than the initial prep work would take. For Jonathan (and all of us!), time is money; the more time spent with the Smiths is less time he has to spend with other clients originating additional loans. By preparing the Smiths to bring ready documentation to the first appointment, he can clear discrepancies before the process begins.

Aside from a preparation ethic, Jonathan also lacks the will to make the process better for everyone involved. He has confidence in his own ability to solve any problem, so he chooses to be reactive and isolated. To bring true value to the company, Jonathan needs to do more than just close deals and solve problems as they happen. He needs to consider both his clients and his teammates before taking action.

For Jonathan, pragmatism would be more effective than optimism. If he makes the initial investment of time and effort to identify potential roadblocks with each client, he can close more deals sooner, and leave more time for solving actual (rather than self-inflicted) crises. A simple recheck of the deal criteria with the lender's representative in the beginning would save pain and suffering for all involved.

Moreover, if Jonathan proactively keeps track of lender guidelines, he would not only resolve issues before they happen, but also be a resource for other loan officers in the company. By watching for patterns and anomalies in his deals and lender guidelines, he can actually help the company be more competitive by increasing their funding average.

On the client side, Jonathan puts the company's reputation at risk. He avoids the difficult conversations with Sean and Rebecca until they are unavoidable—and nearly too late. Managing their expectations consistently along the way would alleviate unnecessary stress. Knowing what Jonathan knows, they also could accuse him of misleading them about the likelihood of their approval. Jonathan is very lucky it worked out.

If you want to create value for the company, you must:

1. Become the expert in all you touch.

2. Proactively solve problems before they start.

3. Improve on the capabilities and reputation of the company.

Jonathan, the Valuable Employee

When setting up the appointment with the Smiths, Jonathan gave them a detailed list of everything they needed to bring to expedite their loan. He explained how any inconsistency could delay or endanger the approval, and followed up with an email outlining the information they discussed.

In studying the Smith's loan application and the documentation they brought, Jonathan realized there could be some complications. There were a few small inconsistencies in the paperwork, but together they set a strategy to resolve the issue up front. He also carefully checked the lender guidelines once a week for any updates and realized the most recent change could increase the Smith's required down payment.

At the appointment, Jonathan worked with the Smiths to correct the inconsistencies and helped them answer the questions he anticipated. He asked them to get additional supporting documentation, and together they wrote letters to explain any inconsistencies. He also helped them come up with alternative acceptable ways of producing and documenting the additional down payment cash necessary.

The underwriting process went smoothly: Jonathan was able to answer all the underwriter's questions without going back to the Smiths for more information, and the application went through without a delay. Jonathan was able to close the loan on time, which in turn allowed the Smiths to close their real estate transaction on time. Meanwhile, he identified two more potential loans to fund. When he found out two other underwriters ran into problems as a result of not being aware of the updated lender guidelines, he decided to start a once weekly email to all MCF loan originators that would contain all necessary updates so they would be aware, too. The Smiths were so pleased with the ease of the process that they recommended Jonathan to several of their friends.

3 Value Steps
Employees Can Take Today

To be truly valuable, you need to focus on delivering substance over style. You do this with careful thought and solid preparation. Aim to be thought of as someone who knows the right stuff, does their homework, and can calmly tackle any situation without leaving a trail of destruction in their wake. The easiest way to do that is to find and solve issues before they become problems—creating a drama-free environment for customers and employees.

It doesn't matter if it's your whole company, your division, or just your job. Those who can identify potential hazards and remove them systemically will always rise to the top. Worry less about how the labor is "supposed" to be divided, and more about how to produce the optimal result. Focus on one of these three problem-removing strategies:

1. Take things apart.

Don't take anything for granted. Learn everything you can about why things are the way they are. Practice de-constructing how things work. The more you understand the inner workings of formulas, processes, and mechanics, the more you can identify where breakdowns might occur. Ask why—five times. Often, you'll get an answer along the lines of, "That's the way we always have done it"—which may mean it's ripe for improvement.

Look for anomalies and point them out. You may ruffle a few feathers with your inquisition, but you'll be the one to bring the issues and solutions to the surface, and the people up top will thank you later.

2. Create a diligence process.

Every job is different, but all require some aspect of information gathering. Build a standard process for preparation, along with a checklist for completion. The commercial airline industry has a stellar safety record because all mechanics, flight attendants, and pilots follow detailed checklists. We suggest you read *Checklist Manifesto* by Atul Gawanda. Wherever there is smoke, there is fire—drama—and that calls for a checklist. Strive for a drama-free environment that doesn't rely on heroics to save the day, i.e., pilots miraculously navigating a daily crisis (none of us would fly!).

Actively pursue information through company resources such as the company intranet and industry publications. Ask people in other departments to explain how things work so you understand where you fit in the process and who else is affected by your actions.

3. Reduce "division of labor."

Look for areas where you can reduce the number of people who touch a process. Last century's idea of "division of labor" is less effective in today's environment. Harley-Davidson replaced their assembly line with small teams that assemble an entire custom cycle, resulting in better quality, faster assembly, and more engaged teams. Mortgage firms and other professional service organizations are cross-training people so one or two can handle a process that had required five people. This also adds variety to what can become a monotonous job.

Relay races are usually lost because of mishandled handoffs of the baton. Eliminate as many handoffs as possible to avoid the need for heroics to save the race.

Create Immediate Value Today

- **If you read nothing else, read…** *The Problem with Saying "Don't Bring Me Problems, Bring Me Solutions"* Harvard Business Review article by Sabina Nawaz.

- **If you watch nothing else, watch…** Atul Gawande's TEDTalk "The Importance and Value of the Checklist."

- **Start the conversation! Here is a practical tip:**

  - **For you:** Where are you and your colleagues experiencing the most drama in your work? Speak up!

  - **For your leader:** Ask your team where they are experiencing the most drama right now. Convene a team and use the "5 Whys" technique to get to the root of the problem and create/update a checklist if needed.

Want more inspiration?

Find more resources on this habit, including expert advice from Growth Institute thought leaders, at *ScalingUp.com/Valuable_Employee_Resources/*

Habit 8
Improving Process

Mary sat at her desk, listening as her four very stressed-out coworkers complained. Mary ran the visual communications department for Excelsior Marketing, a growing digital agency.

"We're completely swamped," said Nijo. "Since the company newsletter told everyone there's an in-house video team, all the department heads want us to do internal projects for them! Now we have to fit in everyone's requests on top of the external projects that actually bring in revenue for our division."

Zak chimed in, "We've gotten five new requests this week, but we're not caught up with our current client projects or the four internal requests we got last week. We're all working late every night and on weekends. And we can't say no without offending some leader or other. Mary, you've got to get them off our backs."

"I can see you're really feeling the pressure," Mary replied, adding a sympathetic smile. "How many hours are you spending on each one?"

All four chimed in at once, describing multiple projects where they had already put in 40-plus hours.

"Can you tell me about your process?" she asked. "What are your action steps for a new project?"

Mary got several seconds of blank stares before Austin finally said, "Well... we pretty much take them case by case. I mean, each one is different. But we always start with a two-hour meeting with the whole team. Then we assign tasks and get to work. But it never ends, and we are buried."

"Well, I appreciate your dedication," said Mary, "but maybe we can find ways to help you work more efficiently. Let's take 30 minutes to identify the actions that all projects have in common. Then maybe we can simplify the process. Emily, you haven't had a chance to share. Why don't you start?"

In the end, it took Mary over two hours, but she helped the video team come up with a checklist of steps that every project had to include. She had them estimate how much time each one might take, depending on the complexity of the project.

There were some tense moments, especially with Zak and Nijo, who had the most technical experience and felt that a non-tech person like Mary probably couldn't fully understand their work and were therefore hesitant to share details. But in the end, they managed to agree on a general structure that would streamline planning and assign responsibilities to divide the work more evenly.

Mary admitted to herself the new system wouldn't exactly be a finely-tuned machine. The group didn't have time to design an effective system to track the projects, and there were probably even more steps common to every project they hadn't identified. There also wasn't any sort of quality assurance process. Actually, she thought, there were probably a thousand other things they could have considered with more time. But the team needed to get to work right away, and they just couldn't afford to waste any more energy on this effort. The process would develop and mature with time.

Generally, Mary was pleased with what they figured out, and it was certainly better than the total lack of process they had before. With the new system in place, it looked like the video team would be able to manage the regular load, if barely. Sensing there still would be overload initially due to the backlog, Mary agreed to dedicate additional evening time in the coming weeks to pick up the slack herself until the team caught up.

After the meeting, the team seemed more relaxed and more confident they could weather through the crunch and survive the future. Before she left that day, Mary sent an email to the other departments requesting that the video team be given more time on internal project requests. Then, she treated herself to a well-deserved latte as she prepared for a late night.

Taking Mary
from Adequate to Valuable

Mary appears to be a solid front-line team leader. She obviously cares for her people and is adept at problem solving to make sure things get done. She is even willing to pitch in herself to make happen what needs to happen. But her quick fix approach leaves her division—and the company—susceptible to breakdown at any moment.

Mary helps by creating a temporary solution that identifies a rudimentary system and prioritizes actions. But this new video division needs sophisticated systems and processes that can support the long-term needs of the company. The team needs to approach the workload in a completely different way. And most importantly, it needs to do it with the resources it already has.

Even Mary's seemingly kind gesture of picking up the slack for the next few weeks hides a darker reality. She's simply masking a systemic problem, instead of continuing the discussion with the video team and addressing concerns with senior leadership.

Mary allows her team to function in an improvisational manner, creating inefficiency and needless repetition. There are hardly any replicable processes in place, little documentation, and virtually no fail-safes. Any hiccup or loss of a team member could result in total failure.

Mary solves for a quick crunch but does little to ensure consistency and continued department profitability for the company. Instead, she creates longer-term problems and leaves the company open to systematic failure down the line.

For Mary to bring real value, she needs to help the team develop scalable processes that can be taught, measured, and improved. She needs to make sure team members are cross-trained so they can succeed even if someone is absent. And she needs to encourage her team to view everything from the perspective of possible future improvement.

Finally, she should create regular opportunities for ongoing team input.

The video department needs to dedicate serious time and brain power to developing a replicable, efficient process. One hour of planning time up front could save multiple hours for every team member on every project in the future. Imagine the exponential impact if Mary requires the team to spend time developing systems and processes rather than simply doing what's in front of them at the moment.

Thinking with a long-term view, Mary and her team can visualize all the elements that make up each project and the many ways the team members might reimagine those steps. Even without the highly technical knowledge of Zak and Nijo, she can assess the talents of the team and help them create systems that get the highest and best use out of each member, while also accounting for redundancy. Additionally, she can help them establish metrics on processes so they can constantly work towards improvement. Then she can evaluate whether the department could be functional and profitable in the long term and communicate her findings to company leadership.

If you want to create value for the company, you must:

1. Examine each process with a long-term, scalable view.

2. Establish metrics that drive efficiency and efficacy.

3. Openly align your processes with the company's.

Mary, the Valuable Employee

When she heard the team's complaints, Mary understood she needed to help them prepare for the future, and fast. She took several hours that day to guide the team as they set up a rudimentary process that identified and streamlined common tasks, divided labor, and tracked each project from beginning to end. It was basic, but it would help them get through this transition period. Then she asked them to set aside half an hour every day for the next several weeks. They would meet as a team and design a totally new video creation process.

Mary explained that it would be efficient, replicable, organized, and transparent. It would be fair to each member of the team and would make the process easier for the customer, whether internal or external. It would also have built-in checks to avoid mistakes and ensure high quality. It would be well-documented, allowing each team member to know exactly what was expected of them and easing the onboarding of new team members. Finally, it included some basic cross-training to allow for greater versatility and redundancy.

The video team initially seemed hesitant about devoting so much time to planning when they had so much work to do. After all, time is money. But Mary assured them this was actually the most efficient way forward: all the planning now would pay exponential dividends in the future. While it cost money and delayed work to hold these meetings, it was an investment in the team's (and the company's) future. Mary made sure the leadership team and the other divisions understood these short-term challenges.

After several weeks of discussion, brainstorming, experimentation, and adjusting, the video team designed a comprehensive, well-organized, efficient process. It took advantage of the strengths of each team member, while also accounting for predictable events like staff vacation and seasonal demands.

The team immediately felt the difference: they communicated better, produced videos more quickly, and were able to work more with the customers to make the videos as engaging as possible. Even with the increased workload from internal and external customers, they produced better videos faster than ever. Inspired by this success, they agreed to meet once per quarter to review their processes and see how else they could improve them.

3 Value Steps
Employees Can Take Today

Reactive thinking and action generally deliver mediocre results. In a sinking boat, mediocre employees scoop out the water. Good employees find the hole and apply a patch; they might even apply a backup patch or hold the patch down themselves. But a truly valuable employee simultaneously asks, "Why do we have a hole in the first place?" They look at the resources on hand and put together a plan to avoid having any additional holes in the future. You can begin to improve processes in your company by trying one of the following:

1. Meet with your peers cross-functionally.

How customers and employees experience your organization (CX and EX) is driven by a set of processes that cut across the various functions in an organization. Yet most workers spend the bulk of their time working with only those in their siloed function.

Have lunch each week with someone from another department and explore how you can better support each other in a shared process. Building cross-functional relationships makes it easier to get to the root causes of problems, helping everyone eliminate wasted effort and needless frustration.

2. Establish clear metrics for each process.

Processes are generally measured three ways: quality, time, and cost. Learn what these are for each of the processes you touch as part of your job. Then calculate your contribution to each (how much time you spend, what your costs are, including your labor, etc.). You know inputs and equipment cost money, but remember each person has an hourly rate of cost as well.

When designing a system or process, calculate the actual costs that will be required, including the value of people's time. Make sure the total cost is appropriate to the value and revenue created at the end. Having the whole video team in planning meetings was likely an expensive proposition, but they used the meetings to increase the efficiency of the production process many times over, which made the meetings economically worthwhile.

Verne details in *Scaling Up* how Ashiana Housing brought together, monthly, their 70 team leads representing every function in the organization (sales, construction, security, maintenance, etc.) for a day of learning and process improvement. Though quite costly, the decisions made at the very first one-and-a-half-day meeting paid for the next ten years of monthly meetings. The second meeting paid for the following ten years!

3. Contribute to process improvement.

Most anything worth doing in a company will likely need doing again. Document each process that is created so others can learn from your successes and mistakes. Find ways to simplify even the complex.

At office furniture manufacturer Steelcase, all 3000+ manufacturing employees regularly contribute "2-Second Lean" videos (taken with their phones) documenting ways they've improved a specific activity or process. A YouTube-like internal site provides everyone with searchable access to these videos, which contributed to reducing defects by half.

Each month, ask everyone on your team to contribute an idea that will improve the quality, speed, and cost of something they do. These small improvements add up to creating a much easier job for everyone while benefiting the customer and company.

Create Immediate Value Today

- **If you read nothing else, read...** *The Goal: A Process of Ongoing Improvement* by Eli Goldratt. Verne considers it the best business book ever written.

- **If you watch nothing else, watch...** "4 Inspiring TED-Talks about Lean and Continuous Improvement."

- **Start the conversation! Here is a practical tip:**

  - **For you:** What is one thing that could be easier in your job or for the customer? Lead a team to find a solution based on what you read and watched above.

  - **For your leader:** Survey your team, asking them three questions: What should the team/company

1) start doing, 2) stop doing, and 3) keep doing? Publish the results back to the team (unless there is a personal attack on someone) and then take action on one of the start or stop issues.

Want more inspiration?

Find more resources on this habit, including expert advice from Growth Institute thought leaders, at *ScalingUp.com/Valuable_Employee_Resources/*

Habit 9
Getting Things Done

BreezeAir Heating and Air Conditioning was having a crazy year, and Dylan was more stressed out than ever before. The consumer-oriented HVAC company ran a very successful promotional campaign, and business was booming. The technicians, though, struggled to keep up with the schedule. Installations and repairs often went over the scheduled time slot, making the technician late for the next appointment. As leadership would not approve overtime, Dylan and his customer service team frequently had to reschedule two to three appointments at the end of a day. Their online reviews showed customers were not happy about the service, and the company was at risk of losing all the ground it had gained in recent months.

Dylan hated that customers and employees seemed to be at war. Each blamed the other for problems and delays, and the technicians often complained about the rude comments they endured from homeowners. That's not how it was supposed to be. The company's tag line promised so much more: "Fast and Friendly, Your Home's Best Friend!"

BreezeAir had efficiency procedures, but many of the technicians and phone representatives didn't seem to know them, or at least didn't use them. With their current training system, it would take months to refresh every employee on the best, quickest ways to make needed repairs.

Dylan thought maybe he could help the customer relationships, however. First, he got permission to bring in temps and clear the schedules of the phone representatives and technicians for a day. He catered in coffee, donuts, and lunch, and delivered eight hours of training. They reviewed procedures for late arrivals and unexpected cost overruns. He had everyone role-play encounters with difficult customers and coached them on ways to diffuse a tense situation. At the end of the day, Dylan tested everyone's knowledge with an online quiz. Further, he implemented a standard survey where customers could evaluate employees on elements such as friendliness and politeness.

Next, he created a shadow program where the company's best-liked, most outgoing employees could show the shy or less social ones how to interact with homeowners in a positive way. Finally, he convinced leadership to add a little extra time to each appointment. It meant a bit less income in the short term, but far fewer late arrivals and reschedules.

Slowly, BreezeAir's online feedback and customer survey results started to improve. Dylan's supervisor made a point of highlighting their higher Angi rating at the quarterly meeting. Both technicians and phone reps seemed happier and less stressed. BreezeAir was getting back on track as the Home's Best Friend.

Taking Dylan
from Adequate to Valuable

Dylan clearly takes BreezeAir's tag line to heart and wants the best for both his fellow employees and their customers. His earnest efforts help turn around a bad situation and improve customer relationships in a meaningful way… for now.

Dylan should try to make sure the training he sets up goes beyond just the scheduled single day. Dylan's efforts to improve employees' people skills do make things better for BreezeAir's current staff, but it isn't a long-term solution. Eight hours of training might not be sufficient for some employees. Plus, new hires won't benefit from this one-time training. Dylan should work with company leadership to integrate his training into the onboarding program for new hires. He could even create some testing to include in the initial interview process to weed out candidates without certain people skills. Then, Dylan could make a business case to convince leadership of the necessity of regular refresher training.

It's clear company leadership isn't seriously examining the customer or employee experience. Their reluctance to make even minor changes to schedules is short-sighted, and they seem clueless about the obvious need for remedial and ongoing employee training. Still, Dylan misses a chance to shine a light on these opportunities for the company. He should gather and present metrics that illustrate the hidden costs of constant rescheduling and inefficient mechanical processes. Valuable employees don't assume their company will recognize every problem without someone to point them out.

Dylan's well-executed eight-hour training program and newly-lengthened appointments put a temporary band-aid on some existing customer service problems. Unfortunately, the biggest problem remains: the staff is still unable to solve mechanical problems efficiently. Dylan understands the limitations of the company's existing training system, yet when permitted a day of training, he makes no attempt even to touch the efficiency issue.

Dylan knows how the problems started: employees were not implementing the company's efficiency procedures on repairs. But he doesn't dig deep enough to find out why there was a lack of accountability in the first place. Dylan would be wise to determine whether there is a lack of motivation to follow the efficiency procedures. Why don't the techs prioritize proper technique? Perhaps techs are never properly trained on them in the first place. Perhaps leadership is incentivizing the wrong behavior. Maybe the techs disagree with the recommended procedures. Dylan needs to explore this issue and uncover root causes. He should find opportunities to engage with the techs to learn what they do and why.

In the long term, it seems likely things will regress back to how they were in both customer service and efficiency. This is because Dylan does not establish any consequences for failing to maintain desired behaviors. Customer ratings and maintenance efficiency records are not tied to any incentives or punishments. Dylan should lobby company leadership to establish reporting mechanisms and appropriate rewards in the process to ensure that good work always continues.

If you want to create value for the company, you must:

1. Help establish and participate in ongoing *training* for required activities so others (including customers and fellow

employees) aren't negatively impacted by someone who doesn't know what they are doing.

2. Make sure people have the *structure*, *processes*, and *tools* they need to get things done.

3. Support meaningful *consequences* for those who can't make the grade.

Dylan, the Valuable Employee

Dylan understood he had two jobs: improving the customer experience and making the techs more efficient. He convinced company leadership to allow him to conduct a comprehensive day-long training for all staff members where they reviewed efficiency procedures, conducted role playing exercises, and practiced de-escalation strategies. He provided techs and phone reps with binders that included all procedures, helpful reminders, and scripts they could use when dealing with the most frequent issues. He also created a shadow program in which their best phone reps and techs would mentor new and struggling team members so everyone could benefit from the seasoned operators' experience.

While he felt this training program was a good first step, Dylan understood existing staff would need refreshers and new hires would need initial training. He created a full-day training program for new hires that covered much of the same material as the one-day training. He then convinced leadership to allow him an additional half day per quarter where he could conduct maintenance training for all staff. They would review efficiency procedures, conduct post-mortems on actual mechanical problems and customer inter-actions, and discuss customer satisfaction metrics from the prior quarter. He involved top performers in the planning and execution of these sessions, and made sure to highlight to the whole group the employees who showed the most improvement.

Finally, Dylan tackled the efficiency of the HVAC techs. He conducted small group discussion sessions to evaluate the status of their training, to determine whether there was a motivation or consequence issue that needed correction, and to learn how the techs thought their procedures might improve. He discovered the company's onboarding training was great at teaching the techs how to diagnose problems but wasn't nearly as effective in teaching them how to solve those problems. Dylan also learned the company's bonus evaluation process did not include efficiency or customer satisfaction as a metric, so the techs were not incentivized to study the efficiency manuals or follow customer service best practices. Dylan was able to fix these problems, and convinced leadership to allow him to conduct quarterly testing on efficiency procedures to ensure techs stayed fresh on their training.

Between the improvement in customer satisfaction and the more efficient HVAC mechanical service, BreezeAir's positive reviews increased substantially, and their online reviews became a steady source of new leads. Their improved training programs, more interactive listening sessions with leadership, and strong relationships with customers also led to increased staff retention. Dylan's determination to get to the bottom of the issues made a tangible contribution to his coworkers' happiness and to the company's bottom line.

3 Value Steps
Employees Can Take Today

Productivity only occurs when people are accountable for the work they take on. Productivity falls apart when people fail to do their fair share. You can encourage those around you to step up with one of these actions:

1. Start with you.
Where are you clogging the system? Examine your job description and evaluate your performance. Identify places where you are unproductive because you are not motivated, you don't have the structure, or there are no consequences if you don't get the task done. Refine your workload and restructure your processes to account for each of those factors. If you establish consequences for yourself, share them with others so they can help hold you accountable.

We recommend David Allen's *Getting Things Done* book and training. From getting your email inbox to zero each day to getting things out of your head and on paper so you don't forget to do something, David details fundamental activities that will increase your personal productivity and simplify your job and life.

2. Emphasize curiosity.

Encourage your team members to look at every process in the company with a critical eye and do the same yourself. What do you notice, good and bad? Do you see inefficiency? Opportunity? Happy employees or dissatisfied ones? And most importantly, why? In fact, ask why five times. Why is this happening? Then why is that happening?, etc.—until you trace it back to the causes. Question what you see, even those things you assume are positive. Talk to everyone involved (why those cross functional luncheons are valuable!) and ask questions, especially of the front-line operators who put the whole process in motion.

3. Set goals each day and week—and exceed them!

It was consultant Ivy Lee who, a hundred years ago, taught the titans of industry to set priorities. Specifically, each night list your and your team's six priorities for the next day. Then sleep on it and wake up to see if they are still the same, adjusting if needed.

The key is to number the priorities from one to six and start with #1. Usually #1 is the toughest (like spending time writing this book!) so we tend to work on the other five first. The discipline is to not move to #2 until #1 is completed.

Do the same thing for weekly priorities. Set what Silicon Valley calls a "sprint": decide the #1 priority for the week, based on what's best aligned with the priorities of your company (ask if you don't know what they are for the quarter or year), and then focus on accomplishing it.

Accomplishing the most important thing each day and each week is the action that will help you get the best results.

Create Immediate Value Today

- **If you read nothing else, read...** *Getting Things Done*, by David Allen.

- **If you watch nothing else, watch...** Jay Papasan's TED-Talk "It's All About Time—Connect Your Someday and Today."

- **Start the conversation! Here is a practical tip:**

  - For you: Make a list, right now, of your top five priorities for tomorrow, then rank them 1 to 5. Tomorrow, work on #1 and don't move to #2 until #1 is advanced.

  - For your leader: At your next weekly meeting with your team, share the number-one priority for the week and what each member can contribute toward completing it.

Want more inspiration?

Find more resources on this habit, including expert advice from Growth Institute thought leaders, at *ScalingUp.com/Valuable_Employee_Resources/*

The key to successful leadership today is influence, not authority.

Ken Blanchard

Part IV

Skills: Habits of Influence

Habit 10: Fostering Communication

Habit 11: Inspiring Creativity

Habit 12: Effecting Change

How does it feel when you are ignored? So much information is thrown into the mix these days it's difficult to get anyone to pay attention to practically anything. Then everyone wonders why mistakes happen or why it's difficult to make any meaningful change.

Most people believe what they have to say is important or useful. And perhaps it is. Just because you have something useful or important to share, however, doesn't make it a priority or even register in the hearts and minds of those around you.

The adequate employee relies upon the existing channels and structures of communication to send messages with the hope that people will engage or at least notice. Sadly, often they do neither.

A valuable employee takes on the responsibility of understanding where people live and how they communicate. They work to expand beyond the norms of basic thought and practicality to inspire others to break out of existing conventions.

You've seen these people. They attract followers. They create movements. They move the ball forward in exciting ways. They don't just wait for the storm to come. They are sufficiently intrigued by the process of growth, so they fire up their imagination to create spectacular futures. When the storm does hit, rather than tamping it down to merely shine as a self-anointed hero, they encourage others with zeal to harness the power of the storm, creating beauty in the calm to come.

The valuable employee has mastered the tools of engagement such as storytelling, humor, and empathy. They understand how to use the media tools of the day to get their message to those who can and will take action. With those tools come responsibility: to create, to be compelling, to be authentic, to entertain, and to be useful.

The habits explored in Part IV are often afterthoughts or left entirely to others, and yet they are the most powerful. They can inspire armies of people to create, grow, and change, resulting in value beyond comprehension.

As you read the following three habits, consider which constraints are restricting creativity, communication, and change in your organization. How can you inspire others to break out of those constraints and create a preferred future for all?

Habit 10
Fostering Communication

Brittany opened the Wednesday meeting with an announcement to her team at Cinemand Software that made everyone's jaw drop: "Bad news, good news. First the bad news: The company still can't prioritize building a communications department at the corporate level. The good news is our team has been asked to be involved more with internal communications. So, since we don't have a marketing/communications department, Customer Service is going to be building the CEO presentation Steve will give at the company's upcoming annual retreat."

"Like, the whole company?" Josh gaped. "All two hundred employees? But... we've never done anything like that. We're a customer service team. PowerPoint's not what we do!"

"The whole company," nodded Brittany. "And Steve has high expectations. He is willing to invest in growing our department if we show we can handle this. Then we get to directly solve some of the communications issues you have been hearing from customers. We need to rock it here if we want a chance at bigger projects in the future."

Fortunately, everyone on the team had pure Type A energy. They had been itching to do more than just answer phones, and they certainly didn't want to wait another year or two to solve customer complaints on communication. They threw themselves into planning for a week solid. They stayed late, watched PowerPoint tutorials, double checked facts and figures, and combed through archives for every relevant detail. They created a respectable corporate PowerPoint presentation—readable fonts, not too many words or animations, and audience interaction.

The next Friday, they reserved a conference room to conduct a test run of the presentation. They invited Steve's assistant, Janna, to watch. It went perfectly according to plan... except the whole team could see Janna was bored stiff.

"Well," she said, "it's sort of dry. Perhaps it could use some jokes. Remember, Steve loves to use humor in public speaking. You should also consider whether anyone will remember the quarterly targets after hearing this. They didn't stand out at all—but generating enthusiasm for those goals is supposed to be the main point of the talk."

"But everyone already got those in an e-mail," protested Josh.

"True," nodded Janna, "but reinforcement is the point. And I spotted at least five grammar and spelling errors in the slides. I hate to give you more work, but it might be best to start fresh. Imagine yourselves watching the speech. See if that inspires you."

After Janna excused herself, Brittany looked around the room. The team wore, "Oh crap, what now?" expressions—all but Aliyah, who was clearly thinking hard.

"You know," Aliyah said slowly, "I took some theatre classes back in college, and it was all about communicating visually to make emotional connections."

She opened her notebook and began to sketch a new slide layout. She asked Brittany to call up the company's color palette and the newest logo design. "Can we find a way to play on the logo more? Maybe do some image research online." Brittany put Daniel in charge of that. Aliyah went on, explaining how things like color and comedic timing get audience attention.

The team started over. Josh found funny YouTube blooper footage that was a perfect introduction for the "company policy" section. Scanning the company Instagram feed, Beki found some great pictures from prior events to depict the year's client marketing calendar.

Brittany dug in with the team and acted as constructive critic, trying to represent Janna's point of view. It took all weekend, but inspired by some of the techniques Aliyah learned at school, they re-designed every slide and wrote an entirely new script. They even had fun—it was like an art project and acting class combined!

Steve's presentation was the highlight of the retreat. It was engaging, and everyone laughed at all the right spots. Many people were thrilled to see their own faces on the giant screen. The team also managed to have a slide *highlighting the quarterly goals. Overhearing others recap the funny moments over lunch, Brittany was filled with excitement and hope. "We're totally ready for a more high-profile project!" she thought as she drove home. "Still, we should review the quarterly goals e-mail first thing in the morning and make sure our team is on track. Steve needs to see we're on top of everything." She made a mental note to pick up breakfast tacos for the morning meeting. The team loved them, and they deserved a reward.*

Taking Brittany
from Adequate to Valuable

Brittany and her team deserve credit for rising to the challenge after some initial failure. Many employees lose hope when they get negative feedback, especially after putting in a lot of hard work. Some might even try to hand off the project to another team. Watching their colleagues enjoy the show must feel like a great (and well-deserved) pay off.

That doesn't mean Brittany and her team got it right, though. In fact, they only got half the message Janna tries to deliver on the topic of organizational communication. The team manages to bring the fun, but still little attention is focused on what should be the key takeaway—the quarterly goals—despite Janna's explicit instructions. If Brittany asks random audience members to recite the quarterly goals a week or even a day later, could they do so? Likely not. She isn't even sure her own team has them down, yet Janna was clear that those were the most important part of the presentation. This is a major problem—Brittany and her team have missed the main purpose!

Brittany is not totally at fault here. She is putting a bandage on a gaping wound in the company structure. Employers say they prize great communicators, who often seem to be in short supply, yet the company hasn't invested in a marketing and communications department with real pros to do the job. Steve is also guilty of thinking communication hinges on a single event, and is seduced by the "flash and trash" of humor and good scenery. He should notice the quarterly goals don't get enough airtime or emphasis. It is important to have an attractive, entertaining medium for your message—audiences don't want to be bored by a dry lecture! But that's only one element of successful communication. Company leadership clearly needs to be educated on creating the kind of systemic focused messaging required to drive key goals. Steve chooses form over function.

Brittany and her team show grit when they commit to improve their work—despite the initial argument that PowerPoint "is not what we do"—but good communication is not a one-time or one-channel event. She should have them craft multiple channels of communication for reinforcement.

Brittany puts too much stock in a single event and a single presenter. If a message is important, it bears repeating. External communication such as advertising relies on multiple exposures for absorption. Although it's often neglected, internal communication requires the same. Brittany should have her team create both pre- and post-event campaigns over the course of the quarter that connect with everyone in the company to reinforce the important takeaways.

When you have a message to send, there are multiple media choices for getting it across. Most of them are relatively easy and inexpensive to produce. Many can be done on a smartphone. It's important to choose the right one (or ones!) based on your audience and their communication habits. Anyone in charge of communication should have enough knowledge to know which is the right fit and how to use it effectively. If Brittany really wants to step up and take on the marcomm aspects of the company, she and her team need to master *all* elements of communication: the content *and* the mechanism.

Additionally, good writing skills still count, even in this age of artificial intelligence, predictive text, and spell check. Grammar and spelling mistakes, misuse of punctuation, and improper word choice all create a negative impression of the writer and presenter. If Janna doesn't catch them, it's likely the team's typos make it all the way to the boss' desk—and possibly even to an auditorium full of their colleagues.

Brittany failed to apply a high standard to the work product before it went out the door.

Consequently, Brittany makes her colleagues happy for now, but falls short of meeting the company's communication needs.

If you want to create value for the company, you must:

1. Craft each communication around its key takeaway.

2. Master the various mechanics and styles that form memorable content.

3. Create planned messaging campaigns that go beyond a single event or person.

Brittany, the Valuable Employee

Brittany embraced Janna's feedback and rethought her approach. She now understood her team's job wasn't just to create a fun presentation—it was to leverage communication tools to help company personnel make the quarterly goals an ongoing priority. She needed to create an emotional connection that would make the goals stick in their minds.

Brittany had Aliyah put together a quick tutorial for the team on what she learned about communication in theatre. Aliyah gave them the highlights on body language, verbal cues, and persuasion. She also discussed big picture thinking: that every element of the program should serve the main purpose of reinforcing the quarterly goals.

Brittany told her team to analyze this internal company audience just like they do their external customer audience. They brainstormed how to frame the goals in a compelling way that would fit into the context of the rest of the presentation. They decided to have Steve tell a funny story about a fictional employee whose antics laid out and explained the quarterly goals. Daniel redesigned the slide deck while Josh and Beki found pictures and videos that would complement the other sections of the presentation. Then they wrote the story together and included suggestions for Steve about body language and verbal pacing. They also printed flyers advertising the coming presentation and hinting at the fictional employee's journey through the quarterly goals. Finally, they took pictures of Steve with props that alluded to how the story explained the goals, and posted them after the retreat. They also provided Steve and Janna with copy and images for engaging supplemental emails that could go out weekly to reinforce the message launched at the meeting.

Steve's presentation was the highlight of the retreat, and with good reason. It was fun, engaging, and really set up the employees to remember the goals. Steve was particularly delighted with Brittany's team; they seemed to really grasp the importance of consistent and engaging messaging, and he decided to put them in charge of the next quarter's entire suite of internal marketing.

3 Value Steps
Employees Can Take Today

Valuable employees prize great communication and cultivate their skills. Experiment with one of the following steps:

1. Focus on the key message.
When planning a communication, don't force the main message into a pre-determined format. Instead, begin with the end in mind. What is the most important thing for the audience to take away? How will they most easily consume and retain that information? Make that the center-piece of the communication and design the rest of the presentation to support that main point. The main idea combined with audience habits should guide your choices on format, tone, and reinforcement steps.

2. Expand your communication repertoire.
According to a 2016 Pew Research study, employers' number-one desired skill in employees is the ability to write. All of today's com-munications mediums start with good writing and then an ability to articulate verbally. Your long-term value is limited without these skills. Local colleges and universities offer short writing courses for

professionals; these can also be found online. A good instructor will help you firm up your grasp of the mechanics and the rules of usage. They can also coach you on style so your writing becomes clear, easy to understand, and reader-friendly.

Then join Toastmasters, an organization with local chapters in almost every city and online communities, which helps you practice public speaking, improve your communication, and build leadership skills.

3. Design a campaign in a variety of formats.

There are several choices for every class of communication: *text*, *audio*, *visual*, and *live*. People expect to receive communication in a variety of formats, and you need to connect with them where they live. Whether communicating through PowerPoint, video, podcasting, blogs, or e-mail, there are proven practices for each that can be learned with effort and repetition.

With so many choices and so much competing content, it can be intimidating using a new communication method for the first time. But you don't have to start from scratch. What are the award-winning articles, podcasts, videos, commercials, etc., in your industry? Spend time viewing these on a regular basis. Take notes on the content. Subscribe to the newsletters, blogs, or podcasts from the most respected thought leaders in your field and study them. Watch TEDTalks with friends or colleagues and discuss the techniques the speakers use to get across their most important points. Dissect what makes them engaging and their message memorable. The next time you have to share a message, design your campaign in the style of one of the experts you've researched.

Create Immediate Value Today

- **If you read nothing else, read...** *Stories That Stick* by Kindra Hall.

- **If you watch nothing else, watch...** Marcus Alexander Velazquez's TED Talk "The Art of Effective Communication."

- **Start the conversation! Here is a practical tip:**

  - **For you:** Join Toastmasters—which has virtual options.

  - **For your leader:** Give your #1 priority for the quarter/ year a theme name, perhaps a favorite movie or song. All military missions (and movies and books) have a name—yours should as well to make it memorable.

Want more inspiration?

Find more resources on this habit, including expert advice from Growth Institute thought leaders, at *ScalingUp.com/Valuable_Employee_Resources/*

Habit 11

Inspiring Creativity

Everyone at BrightStart-4-All was excited to have a full-time marketer join the team—no one more so than the director, Ramon. The non-profit, which focused on underserved Latinx babies and young children in a major metropolitan region, had begged the board for three years to fund the new position, and the board had finally responded. Ramon and the others would no longer have to make do with summer interns or well-meaning volunteers. The new marketer, Connie, was smart, energetic, and bilingual. She grew up in the inner city and knew the local area. Her previous employers all praised her social media-savvy approach. Having Connie around could be a complete game changer for fundraising and awareness.

Connie hit the ground running, too. First, she created a full complement of social media profiles—Facebook, Twitter, Instagram, the works. Ramon was amazed at how tirelessly Connie worked, coming in early and staying late.

"You must be exhausted," he said one Friday.

Connie shrugged cheerfully, "Well, nobody else really knows how to work with Instagram or Twitter. And they only know enough about Facebook to see pictures of their grandkids. So, it's up to me. But I don't mind. It's fun! And I think it's really going to make an impact."

Next, Connie convinced the board to fund an update for the website.

"We can use the same template I used at my last job," she promised. "We'll just change the wording and pictures. That will help keep costs down." The new look was fresh, modern, and promoted their social media channels. Every part of their print materials and web presence now featured new, adorable pictures of the babies that BrightStart-4-All served. Connie took many of them herself, which also saved money.

The changes came a bit hard and fast for some, without a great deal of warning or explanation. But even the old school employees had to admit the new materials looked great. Connie's bubbly energy was infectious, too, and she soon became popular with everyone. Ramon was glad to hear the positive comments rolling in:

"She takes care of everything!"

"She's so artistic! I could never be that creative!"

"She's like a one-woman army!"

The whole office was excited to see their social media accounts add new fans and followers each week. The online donation platform worked well, too. Despite initial fears that older donors wouldn't convert to the new system, giving numbers held steady.

Not every idea succeeded, of course. The "Local Baby" Christmas cards only sold moderately.

"Ah, well," Ramon consoled her, "Our Lady of Charity has used cards as their big fundraiser for decades. Maybe the market is saturated." The Kickstarter project to remodel the 20-year-old playroom at the clinic had fizzled out, too. In response, Connie created an online survey, discovering that the current donor pool felt giving fatigue after the organization's recent capital campaign.

Things got tense for about a month when Connie suggested changing their e-mail newsletter template. One of the board members had designed it, and other staff had not wanted to make a fuss.

"Don't poke that bear. Just leave the e-mail alone," she was advised. But Connie persisted. She invited the board member out for coffee, explained the reasoning behind the change, and got buy in. She re-designed the template to be much simpler and easier to read. By the end of the year, their open rate for e-mails had gone up 5%, to everyone's great surprise.

At the annual party, a special toast to Connie was made, celebrating the success of her first year.

Taking Connie
from Adequate to Valuable

Connie tries to bring a creative approach to her work. She works to impact the company's image in a more creative and effective light, and within the bounds of the limited resources of a non-profit. Admirable to be sure, but Connie's success is narrow. BrightStart-4-All hopes Connie will "be a complete game changer for fundraising and awareness"—yet the only measurable impact from her work is a 5% increase in email open rates and some new social media accounts. The number of donors, amount donated, and number of needy children served all remain the same, and the Christmas card and renovation efforts do not succeed.

Connie obviously hasn't learned that creativity for its own sake doesn't usually optimize growth. On a practical level, Connie's own creative approach is basic. Adding a few new social media followers each week isn't helping her organization advance in exponential ways. She knows some tools and techniques, but doesn't apply them in creative, highly impactful ways. In the short term, she fills a lot of needs, but she doesn't always do so wisely or to maximum effect. A better sense of marketing and strategy would help expand their donor base into new communities, rather than just help keep the current ones engaged.

There's also no evidence that Connie is getting to know the company's stakeholders—the population that the organization serves and its donors. She is applying the exact same methodology she used in previous jobs, but not all of it may fit this new situation. If Connie deploys the online survey before Christmas, for example, she can use those insights to produce more impactful seasonal marketing. Further, it seems she is only applying her creativity to social media and print materials, without discovering the best way to engage existing stakeholders and recruit new ones.

In fairness to Connie, BrightStart-4-All leadership does not provide the appropriate resources to allow creativity to flourish. While they are excited about hiring a creative, they don't give Connie the support or direction to apply her creative approach to non-creative elements in the company, which would elevate out-of-the-box thinking across the team. While they recognize her solitary efforts, no one bothers to step in to help. Further, Connie shouldn't be the first one to survey existing donors.

Still, to many business folk, marketing that comes in a pretty package can look like creativity. Unfortunately, it may simply be artistry that lacks the necessary practicality. What creativity Connie does bring is limited to her own performance. If she is hired away next week, the company basically would still be in the same boring rut with their communication and thinking; social media accounts and a new email template won't move the needle in a meaningful way.

Efficient creativity doesn't just throw everything against the wall, like the Christmas cards and Kickstarter campaign, to see what sticks. Instead, efficient creativity is tempered by careful research and tapping others' experience.

Connie is hired as the creative, but she doesn't bring her coworkers in to collaborate, which is at the heart of organizational creativity. Connie knows her colleagues don't know how to use social media, but she never bothers to teach them—and in the process misses the opportunity to learn more about her colleagues, their unique abilities, and their creative minds. The feedback Ramon hears is very telling: Connie prefers to be a "one-woman army" who "takes care of everything." If her coworkers truly think they "could never be that creative," Connie hasn't done her job well.

Rather than being the go-to for creative work, Connie should find ways to introduce creative thinking into everyone's activities. By unleashing creative thought into the BrightStart-4-All culture, people will begin to think more broadly about their work even when it doesn't require art or fantasy. By keeping her skills to herself, she limits her colleagues' developmental growth instead of inspiring them to think differently.

Rather than engaging others in the creative process, Connie takes it all on herself. She fails to expose others to her method of thinking or encourage them to engage in and develop their own process. There may be some untapped creative geniuses at the organization, but Connie will never find out if she doesn't encourage them.

For example, getting the ok from a board member to change the e-mail template is fine, but she and the company would be better served to engage the board member in the process, or better yet, to establish a creative process that everyone in the company can apply to their own work.

If you want to create value for the company, you must:

1. Understand precisely what the end goals of the organization are.

2. Apply creativity in practical and expansive ways, rather than solely for the sake of creativity.

3. Actively engage others in the process in order to generate new ideas and get buy in.

Connie, the Valuable Employee

Connie wanted to hit the ground running, but knew she first needed to take stock. She undertook a detailed historical analysis of past marketing strategies employed by BrightStart-4-All and other local non-profits, and also conducted a marketing survey of existing stakeholders. As there had never been a single marketing coordinator before, this required her to talk to the various divisions within BrightStart-4-All, which simultaneously provided the opportunity to learn more about her new colleagues and ask how she could support them. Soon, Connie developed a comprehensive, detailed multimedia marketing strategy that was vetted by every division, including leadership, and had universal buy in.

Connie decided to infuse creativity and fun into the culture. She hosted "lunch and learns" to invite others to explore their own creativity, using fun projects like storytelling and video making related to the company's core values and messaging. This gave her both people and content as resources to create outside media.

Connie then created social media accounts across a number of platforms. She held a series of training sessions on effective social media usage, and each division was then scheduled to create content on a rotating calendar. Using what she learned from her past work experience and drawing on input from every division in BrightStart-4-All, Connie also spearheaded a committee (made up of the most enthusiastic participants from the lunch and learns) that reworked the website and newsletter, giving the organization a fresh, modern look while still meeting the needs of every department and driving their mission. Connie was delighted to find the staff hungry for marketing advice, so she made herself available to meet with staff individually to answer questions and discuss industry best practices. This way there were many supporters and contributors to the growing creativity in the company.

At the annual party, a special toast to Connie was made, celebrating the success of her first year. Connie had overseen a social media launch that was attracting new followers every month and converting them into donors and volunteers. The open rate for newsletters was up 30% consistently. Departments were creating tons of social and website content, allowing them to expand their library of marketing materials broaden their target audiences. Connie's coordination meetings and learning sessions helped align board goals with staff action. The whole organization was running more smoothly, donations were way up, and awareness was higher than ever. Connie really had become the game changer everyone hoped she would be.

3 Value Steps
Employees Can Take Today

If you are hired to be a creative in any organization, you must be prepared to lead others down the creative path toward specific objectives. Valuable employees leverage their skills and interests to grow the company in meaningful ways. You'll need to go beyond your own brain and activity. Dedicate yourself to one of these three methods of driving creativity within yourself and others:

1. Establish clear, data-driven goals.

When engaging your creativity, it is easy to go wild—but if you don't clearly understand the goals of the organization, the creative work will not stick. Don't just ideate. Help the company clearly define its objectives, as this may be new territory for them. Then make sure everyone's ideas are focused on the desired outcome.

You won't know if creative ideas are working unless you measure the base and then follow up on results. Make sure you have the data you need to refine and improve your work. The days of one-and-done campaigns are over. A/B testing and continuous improvement are required to achieve success.

As Jim Collins suggests in *Great by Choice*, "shoot bullets then cannon balls." In other words, test the idea before going all in. One of Verne's clients selected one region to test overnighting all orders at no additional charge to customers, and revenue jumped 60%—then they rolled it out in other regions, to similar effect.

2. Develop a creativity process.

Creativity rarely comes from the same old routine. You should always be looking for and learning about what is new. Join forums, go to conferences, read, visit museums... Expose yourself to a wide array of learning beyond business. Use what you learn to develop a method of brainstorming, approaching problems from different angles, and seeking innovative solutions.

Additionally, no one gets everything right the first time, especially when innovating. Nothing says you are committed to success and collaboration like having a clear process for feedback at the end of a project. Make sure everyone is reminded of the goals so you can determine the data that shows what worked and what didn't. We encourage you to read fighter pilot James Murphy's book *Flawless Execution* and the importance of structuring an after-action review like the military does after each mission.

3. Surface the creativity around you.

You never know where the next great idea will come from. Will Vinton Studios, creator of many award-winning animation icons (The California Raisins, the M&M characters, etc.), was able to increase the studio's productivity tenfold by having creative artists meet every day for a half-hour "show and tell." Each day one of the creative teams would highlight something clever they had figured out and pass it along to the other teams.

If you want your creative work to be well received and implemented, help your colleagues understand the creative process. Give them clear points to check in and give feedback. A great creative can identify and share compelling stories that are rooted in the core values of the organization.

One specific activity we recommend is attending a trade show in an industry as different as you can find from your own. You can usually walk the tradeshow aisles at no cost, looking at the new ideas permeating a different industry—some of which might be useful in yours! After all, good artists borrow; great artists steal!

Create Immediate Value Today

- **If you read nothing else, read...** *Creativity, Inc.* by Ed Catmull.

- **If you watch nothing else, watch...** Alan Iny's TEDTalk "Reigniting Creativity in Business."

- **Start the conversation! Here is a practical tip:**

   - **For you:** Embrace doubt (Alan Iny's talk). Doubt that the way you've done things will always work. Pick one thing you do on a regular basis and find a better way.

- **For your leader:** Schedule regular "show and tell" meetings with your creatives on the team. Let them show off new ways of doing things.

Want more inspiration?

Find more resources on this habit, including expert advice from Growth Institute thought leaders, at *ScalingUp.com/Valuable_Employee_Resources/*

Habit 12
Effecting Change

Auggie was excited to start his new job at GoGas, where he would lead the engineering team at the gas station chain's corporate office. His team of ten was filled with veterans, most of whom had been with the company for years, even decades.

The team was welcoming, but Auggie knew he had big shoes to fill. The prior department head, who retired after 40 years with GoGas, was beloved across the company and particularly by her team. Auggie understood that newcomers are always viewed with some suspicion; it would take time to earn the team's trust.

As his first task, Auggie set out to learn how the engineering team functioned. When asking questions and observing work, he noticed the GoGas research and development process was surprisingly outdated. He knew there were—and had experienced at prior companies—far more efficient ways of accomplishing the same goals of identifying and executing station design and fuel delivery improvements. They had good CAD software, but they weren't using its full functionality. Further, the way they built their station design models was downright archaic. Other companies were using new, inexpensive technology like 3D printers to quickly and accurately build prototypes, but GoGas hadn't made the switch. Additionally, Auggie was surprised to find they hadn't started to explore how the company would evolve with the electric car market.

GoGas had been in business for several generations and was profitable, so the system was good enough to keep up with competitors. Yet Auggie felt the company was in danger of being left behind by the industry if they didn't start planning for coming changes.

At their next team meeting, Auggie briefed the team on his assessment. He inquired whether the team had ever considered updating their software training or expanding their product lines. The team explained that in the past, they considered making some changes, but it never seemed to be the right time. Any time they got close, some other urgent need or more important priority always came up. They all seemed fairly relieved the changes never went through.

"The company is meeting all its expansion and revenue goals, even exceeding them some quarters," said Ricki.

Abel added, "If it ain't broke, don't fix it, right?"

Auggie understood their reluctance, but believed it was his responsibility to prepare the company for the future. After all, the ownership team brought him in to modernize, and promised him the resources necessary to get the job done. Auggie called a team meeting and announced his decision to train the team on fully utilizing their design software and to invest in 3D printing capabilities. He also told them they would begin the process of adapting to electric vehicles. He explained that these changes would put GoGas on the cutting edge of technology, strengthen and expand their customer base, and position the company for future growth.

Auggie looked around and noticed some skeptical faces. Soon, Chris spoke up.

"Look Auggie, I get where you're coming from here. And I agree we could stand a few changes. But what you're proposing is a pretty dramatic shift. What if we just get the CAD software training and 3D printer for now?" Chris offered. "Let's hold off on the electric product expansion."

Then Abel chimed in.

"Adapting for electric is going to be a massive amount of work. And there's no reason to believe that gas motors are really going anywhere in the near future. We'll still need gas for a long while. Making the switch to electric too soon could really stretch resources." That statement got nods from the rest of the group.

Auggie paused to think. He knew they needed to make changes, but perhaps a gentler approach was warranted. If he could negotiate with the team to find a halfway solution, they could still make improvements. He would be able to move the team towards modernization, and the team would feel like their new boss really respected their opinions. A win-win!

Auggie said, "You know what? I like it. Let's dig into the details."

Over the course of a few more meetings, Auggie and the team worked out a schedule for software training. Using the software more effectively would better prepare them to adapt to electric vehicle needs when the time came. It wasn't a perfect solution, but the team was happy and moving in the right direction. Auggie felt like he took a strong first step towards the modernization he promised.

Taking Auggie
from Adequate to Valuable

Auggie is in an unenviable position: he must lead an entire division into a more modern way of doing business. It's a hard enough task on its own, made more complicated by the fact that there's been little new blood on the team for years. Change can be a challenge.

GoGas leadership hasn't eased Auggie's path to success, either. It's clear company leadership hasn't communicated to employees that change is necessary and happening—now. Whatever growth-minded spirit the leadership team possess hasn't been pushed out to the employees.

Auggie has the right instincts to present his plan to the team and seek their feedback. And really, they don't seem to disagree with Auggie about the necessity of the changes. The source of their pushback is rooted more in their desire to make the changes more slowly than Auggie would like.

Auggie lets down his team and his company. He hasn't illustrated to the team just how dire their situation could become. The company may be fine now, but with the ever-advancing nature of technology and new government regulations, the industry could leave them behind in no time at all. Auggie needs to explain to his team the urgency of getting ahead of the curve rather than playing catch up.

A more valuable employee and better leader would recognize that Auggie needs to affect change by convincing the team to follow him. He needs to make a well supported argument for his plan that explains the details, how they'll achieve the goals, and why the team should want to be involved. He needs to understand how to communicate in a way that changes minds and then gets them excited to be on board.

Dr. Robert Cialdini is perhaps the preeminent expert in the art of convincing. His Seven Principles of Persuasion—reciprocity, scarcity, authority, consistency, liking, social proof, and unity—are proven ways of building consensus around ideas and getting buy in from your audience. Auggie would be wise to heed Cialdini's advice as he approaches the team.

If you want to create value for the company, you must:

1. Understand the root of the problem and craft an effective solution.

2. Be able to communicate the mission in a way that makes others excited to take part.

3. Know how to execute on the plan.

Auggie, the Valuable Employee

Going into the meeting where he would announce his plans, Auggie knew there could be some skepticism from the team. He knew the changes they needed to make, but wasn't sure how to convince his team about them. Auggie researched how to make a strong business case, how to make effective arguments, and how to influence colleagues. He found Dr. Robert Cialdini's Seven Principles of Persuasion and knew he had a path forward.

Auggie designed his presentation to the team with Cialdini in mind. He explained that these changes would put the company in rarified air in the industry—scarcity. He gathered research that proved the effectiveness of CAD software and how 3D printing was revolutionizing engineering R&D—authority. He also found several examples of other companies that underwent changes similar to what he was proposing and included evidence of their success—social proof.

As he planned his presentation, Auggie also anticipated the challenges he expected from the team. He laid a foundation of points they could all agree on, and argued that in light of those facts, his proposal was the most effective way forward—consistency. He knew he would have to engage in some negotiation on the plan, and he was prepared to give on some points so he could gain on others—reciprocity. Most of all, Auggie was glad he'd already put in the work to build relationships with each of his team members, as it would be easier to convince them since they already understood his good intentions—liking.

Auggie's presentation to the team went fantastically. The team shared their thoughts, but instead of the pushback he expected, they asked for more details of the plan and offered constructive feedback. He could tell they were enthused about the future. Using his proposal as the framework, Auggie and the team built a detailed timeline and task list to conduct the software training and begin electric vehicle R&D. The GoGas leadership team was impressed Auggie was able to get such universal buy in so quickly. They were even more impressed when the R&D team started rolling out impressive new station designs that incorporated electric vehicle charging stations, all at a lower development cost and in less time than ever before. Auggie's efforts would play a major role in positioning GoGas for the future.

3 Value Steps
Employees Can Take Today

Valuable employees are able to affect change by communicating their vision, explaining why it is the preferred future, and getting people to back their plan to get there. When you need to affect change, follow this three-step process developed by iconic Zingerman's Deli CEO Ari Weinzweig:

1. *Write an Envisioned Future.*
In a few paragraphs, describe in detail—physically and emotionally— how things will be better when a specific change is made. Changes have included moving the mailbox at Zingerman's distribution center and changing the packaging on a certain type of cheese.

2. Make a List of Everyone Affected by the Change.

In the case of the mailbox, the list would include the people delivering the mail from the post office; the person who will have to physically move the mailbox; the person who will sign off on the expense; and those having to retrieve the mail.

3. Meet with Each Person and Influence Them to Support the Change.

Visit each person on the list and, using Robert Cialdini's Seven Principles of Persuasion, get buy-in from everyone touched by the change that it's good. Then make the change!!

Create Immediate Value Today

- **If you read nothing else, read...** *Influence: The Psychology of Persuasion (New and Expanded)* by Dr. Robert Cialdini.

- **If you watch nothing else, watch...** Derek Sivers' TED-Talk *How to Start a Movement*.

- **Start the conversation! Here is a practical tip:**

  - **For you:** Pick one thing that needs to be changed and follow the three steps above.

  - **For your leader:** Don't do the work for your employees. If someone walks into your office with a problem, they should leave with a project. Have them follow the three steps above.

Want more inspiration?

Find more resources on this habit, including expert
advice from Growth Institute thought leaders, at
ScalingUp.com/Valuable_Employee_Resources/

Next Steps...

Thank you for investing the time and effort to learn about these 12 habits of valuable employees.

The next steps are up to you. Take command of your future. Create real value for your company and advance your career by embracing these 12 habits. And remember to do the job you want next!

The key is one step, one behavior, at a time. Work on one habit/chapter per month, one behavior per week! Mastery is an iterative process.

After you've completed the year-long journey once, repeat it—like accomplished tennis, golf, or pickleball players who go back to the fundamentals with every stroke. You'll find new ways to impact your company's bottom line and your top line. No doubt you'll also gain fans among your colleagues and leaders as you share what you've learned.

If you need a tune-up of a particular habit, rely on the Growth Institute and other resources at the end of each chapter. Use this book as a detailed instruction manual or as a quick reference guide.

Now go be amazing!

The Employer's Guide to Stimulating Value

As we found in our survey of CEOs, employers often have difficulty in finding employees valuable.

So we probed a little further and found that the fault lies not just with the employees, but with the employers as well. Many of the companies lacked the following basic elements:

- Clear standards and values that project company culture
- Detailed job descriptions with metrics
- Solid training programs that help employees define value
- Regular, structured reviews so employees receive useful feedback
- Robust recruiting so poor performers could be replaced.

Often the employer's expectation was that the employee should just "figure it out." Then, of course, the employer would wonder why performance was so inconsistent.

While much of the responsibility should be on the employer to provide the environment and tools to promote and nurture value creation, so often the responsibility ultimately falls upon the individual employee to make up for the employer's lack of infrastructure and effort. This often frustrates the employee who doesn't have a clear understanding of what the employer is looking for.

To help employers be a better partner in value creation, we've created this brief companion guide for today's employers, and those employees rising to the level of employers.

WILL:
HABITS OF DESIRE

Habit 1: Developing Leadership

The more leadership development takes priority, the less leadership will have to spend resources on recruiting, acculturating, and retaining top talent from outside sources. As few as three strategic activities can make a major difference:

1. Deconstruct and share your leadership process as a coach.
Employers have a tendency to assume employees should grow into leaders on their own. Indeed, some leaders do rise thanks to instinctive ability. However, you can't expect every talented person to read your mind and gain all your learning overnight. Think about how and why you do what you do. Keep a journal with your thoughts and share them in one-on-one meetings with employees so they can learn. Don't let daily wins and challenges get lost without extracting the learning value, just like a coach would.

2. Create internal peer learning programs.
If you don't have a formal program, then give up-and-comers direction, budget, and resources to create a system of sharing. Agree to promote it and make sure leaders participate.

3. Apportion time and money to leadership development.
Growth and succession are nearly impossible without developing leadership talent from within. Training a leader can take months or even years. Start small with the resources you have, and grow it over time. Integrate leadership development into performance reviews, and give your employees one leadership challenge every quarter. If you do it right, eventually your homegrown leaders will do it for you.

Habit 2: Aligning Vision

People often don't understand what aligning vision really means. It's not just about getting to a common belief; it's about getting there with a sufficient foundation behind it.

1. Train diligence.

When a company is working to achieve a goal, it's critical that team members understand exactly how to get there. Details matter! Your employee training program should emphasize the importance of diligence in their everyday work. Train them to overprepare and encourage them to pay attention to the details. If they can't do the little things right, they may not be able to do the big things right, either.

2. Focus on truth over expedience.

The right things are not always the easy things. Hard truths can sometimes hurt, but confronting them makes everyone better. Create an atmosphere where employees feel encouraged—even required—to seek out problems and inefficiencies. Maybe things are going fine, but what if they could be way better? You may not even know the opportunity you're missing as a result of complacency.

3. Reward people for digging deep.

It takes mental and physical effort to identify pain points and solve them. Create incentives to embolden employees to get into the weeds. Offer a bonus to employees whose efficiency suggestions save money for the company. Reward enterprising employees with a day off if they're able to solve a recurrent problem. To encourage participation, hold regular meetings with the sole purpose of collecting employee suggestions.

Habit 3: Enabling Growth

It's unrealistic to think that even great employees will just naturally understand how to scale a company. If your company's leadership team is growth oriented, you will need your culture to reflect the same approach. Here are several ways to help all your employees contribute to company growth:

1. Make your plans well-defined and well known.
It's all fine and good to say we want to grow bigger, but an unknown target will cause confusion and disjointed performance. Creating tangible growth objectives—leading to what Collins calls a Big Hairy Audacious Goal (BHAG)—makes growth believable and measurable. Broadcast the goals and incorporate them into daily metrics so employees have a measurable target and can track their progress.

2. Empower employee decision-making.
Create alignment around company decision-making so employees understand how to think the right way on their own. Create a template with your company's specific goals and milestones, and have employees measure their activity against progress towards those ends. You will empower employees to take action with confidence and consistency.

3. Reward forward thinkers by funding safe failure.
In many companies, the tallest blade of grass gets cut. They squash original thinking and suppress innovation. To encourage outside-the-box thinking, employees need a way to safely test innovative ideas before they implement them. Otherwise they will avoid innovation for fear of failure. Apportion time and resources to experimentation and encourage people to spend them liberally. Let them fail gracefully and learn from the experimentation. And reward them handsomely when their ideas succeed!

VALUES:
HABITS OF CHARACTER

Habit 4: Integrating Core Values and Purpose

When Jim Collins and Jerry Porras wrote their 1996 *Harvard Business Review* article "Building Your Company's Vision" about core values, they surely didn't imagine that nearly every company in the world would have a list of five or six phrases posted on websites, wall plaques, and screen savers for all to see... and for most to ignore.

Many companies promote core values and purpose, but few actually integrate them effectively. Kevin relates this example:

75 CEOs attended my Inc. 5000 conference talk about valuable employees. During the course of my talk, I asked, "How many of your companies have core values?" I wasn't surprised to see everyone's hands go up. Then I asked the group to close their eyes, so no one would be embarrassed, and I asked, "How many of you can recite your company's core values?" Only three CEOs raised their hands. All these companies are posting core values everywhere and discussing them in meetings, which is great, but their CEOs don't even know them. And if the CEOs don't know them, how are the employees supposed to live them?

It's one thing to have core values and a core purpose; it's quite another to put them into practice. They must be pervasive and intentionally integrated into your company's processes and procedures, from orientation through advancement. Here are three steps that will make core values truly come alive in your company:

1. Make Core Values and Core Purpose meaningful.
Single words like "integrity" and "trust" don't give much direction to employees on how to make decisions. If a person lacks integrity or trust, telling them to have it will do no good. And having an implied purpose to make the owner money doesn't warm most employees' hearts.

For core values to provide benefit, employees have to understand exactly the behavior the company is looking for. Ask these questions to see if your core values are meaningful:

- Are they actionable?

- Are they measurable?

- Do people understand how to follow them?

- Will they attract talented people you want?

- Will they repel talented people you don't want?

- Can you hire/fire/praise/reprimand based on the value?

- Would you sacrifice profit over this core value?

For a purpose to be effective, it has to answer the question, "What difference are we making in the lives of our people and the world?" Does it warm your heart?

Growth Institute can help you discover the core values that are truly indicative of your culture and define a purpose that resonates with you and your team. Jim Collins' article referenced above also provides several examples.

2. Create Core Values- and Core Purpose-based job descriptions and performance reviews.

The surest way to hire and maintain employees who follow your core values and purpose is to connect it directly to their job requirements. Before you hire, make a list of tangible, measurable requirements that fit with each core value and purpose, and vet candidates against it. After you hire, monitor adherence to core values and purpose and re-move misfits quickly. Companies who hold annual reviews are doomed to suffer through mediocrity for an entire year. Quarterly or monthly reviews offer the opportunity to help employees grow and refine.

3. Recruit heavily.

Companies who don't have a waiting list of ready-to-go, Core Values-compliant recruits are in danger of being terrorized. If you can't replace someone who is useful but toxic, you'll send a message to the rest of the team that your core values and purpose are just for show. Until you build a steady, robust recruiting program, you'll deal with the employees you have or are quickly available, which may not be the ones who fit your values and purpose.

Habit 5: Managing Conflict

Individuals respond strongly to their environment. With intent, employers can create a healthy environment for debate that will move the company forward farther and faster.

1. Train employees to use productive conflict.
Don't assume that all people know how to fight fairly and constructively. Conflict makes many people uncomfortable, but it's essential to success. Allow and encourage employees to disagree with one another, and to vigorously discuss their points of view. Bring in trained professionals who can teach your people how to disagree with one another, debate ideas, and resolve personality struggles.

2. Establish open forums.
The more people practice communication, the better they get. Show them the company wants constant communication by creating infrastructure and regular opportunities for staff to share ideas. Host monthly town hall meetings. Create quarterly surveys. Establish an online suggestion box. Even allow them to vent if they need to.

3. Make sure everyone feels heard.
It's one thing to listen; it's another to let others know that they have been heard. In person-to-person encounters, leaders should practice skills like mirroring techniques, note taking, and follow up questions. For the company at large, explain how you are following up on their ideas, suggestions, and concerns. Track satisfaction statistics and pay attention to what the numbers tell you.

Habit 6: Driving Excellence

Many companies leave excellence to the chance that employees will develop it on their own. Ultimately it may be the employee's responsibility to develop, but employers still play an important role. Companies can support employees by creating learning processes and then holding those employees to higher standards. Providing this structure will empower employees to learn more and do more.

1. Reward learning in new areas.

In a growing company, it's normal for people to stretch into areas in which they're uncomfortable. Build programs to encourage them to go outside of their comfort zones. Have them learn new and advanced skills that will push them and the company to higher levels. In a rapidly changing environment, you'll be glad these skills are in-house.

2. Media-enable your employees.

Nearly all communication today takes place through some form of media. Companies that don't create competencies in multiple media formats will leave people behind, and get left behind themselves. Companies need to be able to communicate effectively to a variety of audiences both internally and externally.

3. Teach planning.

Many companies just expect people to know how to achieve an end goal. They assume people can develop a plan, monitor actions steps and milestones, and account for all the moving parts. Unfortunately, many employees don't have these skills. By creating a standardized structure, employees will know how to communicate with others and how to identify and explain what's missing.

RESULTS:
HABITS OF PERFORMANCE

Habit 7: Surfacing Issues

In his book *Why Are There Snowblowers in Miami?*, Steven D. Goldstein explains how an obvious glitch in Sears' distribution system went overlooked by hundreds of people for years and cost the company valuable resources.

There is a delicate balance, however, between maintaining the status quo and moving reactively to too many ideas, which is why companies often tamp down people who are always bringing up problems and moving for action. Here are ways you can safely and effectively help valuable employees surface issues and solve problems before they happen, without creating chaos in the process:

1. Promote practical ideation and pragmatism.

Idea generation is useful, but not every suggestion is beneficial or appropriate. The wrong proposal can cause distraction or even derail the team. Have the inventor present their idea to the group, and encourage the group to debate its merits. This improves everyone's communication and productive criticism skills, and encourages diligence to ensure the idea has been thoroughly vetted before resources are put at risk.

2. Facilitate information sharing.

A group of people is either equal to or greater than the sum of its parts. To achieve the latter, there must be a constant crossflow of information. Provide the physical, technological, and time capabilities for people from across all departments to share their knowledge with the whole company. Invest in technology that allows your employees to access and share information with ease. Of course, you need to support it with forethought, process, and training so it's not simply a crowded hall closet of meaningless data.

3. Support continual improvement by rewarding solutions.

If you want people to look for new and different ways to make the company grow and be competitive, it's up to you to foster an environment where people are on the lookout for new and better ways to do old things. Be cautious, however, since constant disruption will do just that—disrupt. Innovation is useful only if it results in more profit, so make sure the net benefit is part of a purposeful approach. Create legitimate incentives for finding and solving systemic problems.

Habit 8: Improving Process

Many employers reward people who can solve problems on the fly, when instead they should encourage system builders. Adequate employees solve problems as they happen. Good employees create process for themselves. Valuable employees proactively establish systems and metrics that help the company scale. You can help *them* help *you* with these tips:

1. Encourage process improvement time.

You can't expect people to focus beyond their own immediate issues if you don't give them the time and resources to do so. Establish a budget for people working *on* the business instead of *in* the business. Offer incentives for anyone in the company who can reduce cost or increase capability with systemization. Use technology to make process documentation consistent and abundant. Make documentation part of your onboarding process and incentivize cross-training so people have a reason to review the material.

2. Test potential employees for process capability.

Not everyone can see beyond the work at hand. Give potential hires a chance to show you their ability to solve problems systemically. To know if someone is a good process implementer, give them a small test project and ask them how to make it more efficient for a larger team.

3. Communicate the big picture.

When people are focused on the day-to-day, their approach will be small and immediate. Establishing and communicating a long-term strategy with a Big Hairy Audacious Goal (BHAG) and three-year key thrusts will help employees design systems and processes with the company's end goals in mind.

Habit 9: Getting Things Done

Stuff often doesn't get done when leadership fails to create an environment of accountability. Developing such an environment will increase ownership and improve productivity for everyone.

1. Kill the sacred cows.

"This is the way we have always done it!" is not a good excuse for why your company is saddled with unproductive processes. Encourage your employees to deconstruct the current process so they can find improvement that works for everyone.

2. Incentivize the behavior you need.

Give people the tools and knowledge to perform at their best. Your most unproductive process could linger because what you require and how you reward may conflict. When people don't know how to do something or don't have what they need to get it done, it simply won't be done. Lots of companies are strapped for resources, but training must be a priority. Examine how your metrics and incentives work together so you are getting the behavior you need to succeed.

3. Empower local decision making.

The company must dedicate time and resources to working *on* the business. The people on the ground level know better than anyone how things work. Create safe failure environments where employees can experiment and find better solutions. Give them the opportunity to make decisions consistent with company objectives. Then reward them handsomely and publicly when they do.

SKILLS:
HABITS OF INFLUENCE

Habit 10: Fostering Communication

Companies need great internal communication to succeed, yet most communication dollars are focused on external customers. You can achieve a higher ROI on every dollar you spend communicating with your internal customers. There are plenty of affordable tools today to help make that message stick with the right approach.

1. Create standardized communication standards and protocols.

There are great variations in the ways your employees communicate because there is no required uniformity. Even a simple communication via email can create confusion and eat productivity if there aren't standardized policies regarding what makes a good subject line, how to structure the information, and who should be copied. Establish policies for the length and style of documents like project plans or meeting notes. Standardize your presentation formats so people can focus on the substance of the message rather than the mechanics of delivery.

2. Engage everyone in the communication process.

Avoid making communication a one-way exercise. Rather than scheduling a CEO lecture, create departmental activities that get everyone in on the act. Incorporate communication skills assessments into your hiring and performance review practices. Give them the training and encouragement to use the skills and reward them for effective application.

3. Reward effective creativity.

Often employers are surprised when someone does something different and cool, but it becomes a one-off event that isn't repeated or developed. Establish a practice of elevating unique, entertaining, and effective communication practices. Make sure someone in the company is identifying and replicating the best communications practices across the company.

Habit 11: Inspiring Creativity

Employers who want employees to be creative need to establish environments that support out-of-the-box thinking and action.

1. Provide creative structure that allows for safe failure.

Creative thinking takes time, space, and—perhaps counter-intuitively—specific objectives. If you want different, better thinking, you need to give your team clear goals, ample time, and sufficient resources to brainstorm and otherwise dream before they nail the ideas. Let them know it's safe to experiment. Many people like the idea of being creative, but few have the confidence to risk failure. Establish boundaries that allow people to try new things without putting their livelihood in jeopardy.

2. Get outside guidance and inspiration.

Thinking gets stale without outside input. This is especially true in smaller organizations where there are few creatives. Bring in speakers who specialize in creativity. Send your people to creative conferences, museums, or other creative venues in search of new ideas. Have a session once a month to share innovative thinking from outside the company.

3. Expect more of your creatives.

If you hire creatives and only have them do design work, you are missing a huge opportunity for fresh thinking. Great creatives are taught to see problems in a new way and to bring fresh thinking to old problems. This can apply to the whole spectrum of business, not just to the next piece of media collateral. Expose them to your non-creative staff to get an added boost.

Habit 12: Effecting Change

A lot of companies shy away from teaching their employees to be successful persuaders because they're afraid of the possible repercussions. But companies committed to growth will take that skill seriously. If people in the company can't influence others effectively and for the right reasons, the company will never grow. They need a process to learn how to change hearts and minds.

1. Create a culture where change is welcome.
Employees are less likely to work towards change if the environment doesn't foster it. That tone needs to come from the top. Set and enforce standards on the difference between an argument for argument's sake and effective persuasion. Encourage employees to analyze critically and to find new ways to solve problems. Publicly congratulate those who create something new.

2. Institute a persuasion course.
Require a class on effective persuasion as part of your onboarding programming. Have them learn theories and practice of thought leaders like Robert Cialdini and others. In the safe environment of the class, have them give presentations and create media demonstrating their new skills.

3. Foster strong relationships within your company.
Employees need to be able to communicate effectively with each other, particularly in growth environments where change is constant. Empathy is key here: employees need to understand where others are coming from in order to get their point across while also appreciating their colleagues' needs. Create programs such as cross-departmental knowledge exchanges, take-a-colleague-to-lunch events, inter-department trainings, and after work social events. Provide employees the connections they need to find their followers (see the Derek Sivers TEDTalk we recommend).

Conclusion:
The Power of Caring

Thank you for investing your time in learning how to support your team members in delivering more value for themselves and the organization.

Investing in employee development is a key way to show you care for all stakeholders. Employees delivering more value enhances the customer and employee experience. This, in turn, drives better word-of-mouth marketing for clients and talent. And the organization improves its performance, which allows you to invest more in employee development.

It's a virtuous cycle versus the vicious cycle in which many organizations find themselves. Employees will care better for you, your organization, and your customers if they feel you care for them. That's your number-one job as a leader.

As mentioned earlier, the most important question to ask your employees every week is, "What are you working on, and what's in the way of accomplishing it?" This question best gathers the input you need to know how to coach them. Are they working on the right thing? Is there a process that needs devised or revised? What additional training and development do they need?

Care enough to help them to be amazing!

Author Biographies

Verne Harnish is the founder of the world-renowned Entrepreneurs' Organization (EO), with over 16,000 members worldwide. For fifteen years, he chaired EO's premiere CEO program held at MIT, a program in which he still teaches today.

As the founder and CEO of Scaling Up, a global executive education and coaching company with over 250 partners on six continents, Verne has spent the past four decades helping companies scale up.

A prolific writer, Verne is the author of the bestsellers *Mastering the Rockefeller Habits, Scaling Up Compensation* and *The Greatest Business Decisions of All Time*, for which Jim Collins wrote the foreword. Verne also wrote *Scaling Up (Rockefeller Habits 2.0)*, which has been translated into 27 languages and has won eight major international book awards, including the prestigious International Book Award for Best General Business book.

Verne chairs the annual ScaleUp Summits and serves on several boards, including Vice Chair of The Riordan Clinic; co-founder and chair of Geoversity; and board member of the social venture Million Dollar Women. A private investor in many scaleups, Verne enjoys piano, tennis, and magic as a card-carrying member of the International Brotherhood of Magicians.

Kevin Daum is an entrepreneur, author, and speaker who has engaged and inspired audiences around the globe. A serial entrepreneur with multiple successful exits, Kevin built an Inc. 500 company, where his sales and marketing techniques resulted in more than $1 billion in sales. Kevin is the award-winning author of several Amazon #1 bestselling books. He is the author, co-author, or major contributor to ten books, including *ROAR! Get Heard in the Sales and Marketing Jungle*, *Video Marketing For Dummies, Building Your Custom Home For Dummies, Creativity and Entrepreneurship*, and *12 Lessons in Business Leadership:*